Dr. Sandra Clifton opens her life to tell the story of deception and how she walked into freedom. Many are following the path she has walked. Her insights will help those in captivity as well as leaders seeking to set people free. You will see the effects of culture and how to assist people who are ready to come out of the darkness.

—BILLY JOE DAUGHERTY
Pastor, Victory Christian Center
Tulsa, Oklahoma

Sandra Clifton speaks not only from an academic understanding of the occult, but as a former practitioner. Her insights will inform and transform your life as you learn of the dangers all around us. Her newest work is a must-read for any Christian who is serious about spiritual warfare.

—JAMES TOLLETT, D. MIN.
James Tollett Ministries

FROM NEW AGE TO NEW LIFE by Sandra Clifton
Published by Creation House
A Strang Company
600 Rinehart Road
Lake Mary, Florida 32746
www.creationhouse.com

Unless otherwise noted, all Scripture quotations are from the New King
James Version of the Bible. Copyright © 1979, 1980, 1982 by Thomas
Nelson, Inc., publishers. Used by permission.

Scripture quotations marked NAS are from the New American Standard
Bible. Copyright © 1960, 1962, 1963, 1968, 1971, 1972, 1973, 1975,
1977 by the Lockman Foundation. Used by permission.
(www.Lockman.org)

Scripture quotations marked KJV are from the King James Version of
the Bible.

Cover and interior design by Terry Clifton

Library of Congress Control Number: 2007920195
International Standard Book Number: 978-1-59979-171-5

First Edition

07 08 09 10 11 — 987654321
Printed in the United States of America

From
NEW AGE
To
NEW LIFE

SANDRA CLIFTON

CREATION
HOUSE
A STRANG COMPANY

DEDICATION

TO MY LORD AND Savior Jesus Christ—
all for His glory.

≈

This book is dedicated with all of my
love to my husband Terry, who walked
with me from the pit of darkness into the
light of Christ.

≈

This book is also dedicated to my two
beloved aunts, mighty prayer ministers
and warriors of God—Aunt Bernice
Holden and Aunt Nellie Bacon—who
dared to ask me during my professional
psychic days, "Where is Jesus?"

CONTENTS

~

FOREWORD
by Dr. Paul King

≈

A. W. TOZER HAS DECLARED that the spiritual gift most needed today is the gift of discernment. The New Age movement often operates in the guise of Christian thought; using Christian concepts, Christian terminology, and Christian practices, yet meaning different things. So there is great need for discernment between the genuine and the counterfeit. Sandra Clifton, in her vital, insightful book *From New Age to New Life*, provides that needed discernment. She puts forth the question that began to open her own eyes to the truth: "Where is Jesus?"

I recently heard a prominent minister in the contemporary prophetic movement say that he believes psychics have a gift from God but do not know how to use it properly. This popular misconception claims that psychic abilities are neutral and can be used for good or bad. In reality, such mistaken beliefs can have serious spiritual and emotional repercussions, as Sandra Clifton testifies.

Clairvoyance, extrasensory perception (ESP), and mental telepathy are *not* just other terms for supernatural gifts of the Spirit such as word of knowledge, word of wisdom, or prophecy. Jesus is not the greatest shaman or clairvoyant as some have claimed. Scriptures clearly distinguish that which is spiritual (or Holy Spirit originated) from that which is psychic or soulish in nature:

> But a natural [Greek, psychikos—psychic, soulish] man does not accept the things of the Spirit of God; for they are foolishness to him, and he cannot understand them, because they are spiritually appraised.
> —1 CORINTHIANS 2:14, NAS

> This wisdom is not that which comes down from above, but is earthly, natural [psychikos—psychic, soulish], demonic.
> —JAMES 3:15, NAS

> These are the ones who cause divisions, worldly-minded [psychikos—psychic, soulish], devoid of the Spirit.
> —JUDE 19, NAS

Where do psychic abilities come from? Watchman Nee teaches that Adam was created with paranormal abilities or "the latent power of the soul," but that those abilities became corrupted after the Fall, and thus cannot be trusted. Others suggest that when Adam and Eve's "eyes were opened" after the Fall, they became aware of psychic abilities not intended by God. Both are undoubtedly true. These scriptures demonstrate in either scenario that supernatural entities not from God are behind the use of such paranormal powers.

From her own experiences Dr. Clifton convincingly demonstrates the true nature of New Age thought and practices. She intriguingly shares how God opened her eyes to New Age deception and set her free. This book also presents practical insights for tactful dialogue and prayer for others caught in the web of New Age beliefs. A. W. Tozer believed that you should not write a book unless you have to. This is one of those books that just had to be written.

—Paul L. King, DMin, ThD
Author, Pastor, and Professor of Theology
Oral Roberts University

FOREWORD
by Dr. Kenneth Mayton

~

SANDRA CLIFTON IS PERFORMING a great service to the body of Christ with the publication of her latest book, *From New Age to New Life*. Her journey is a testimony to the grace of God in the life of an individual.

This book can be a great help to pastors and teachers for deeper understanding, to believers as an evangelistic tool, and, to those entrapped in the occult/New Age movement, as a liberating force.

The layout of the book is superb and lends itself as an excellent resource for classes and small groups. The inclusion of prayer strategies and discussion questions is a great plus. This book is both theological and practical.

Sandra brings not only her experiences and testimony, but also an academic/theological background, which is too often missing in topics of this nature. Her book will definitely make a contribution to the current literature available.

Dr. Clifton is an instrument of God for bringing the power of the gospel into today's world. Her dissertation in the Doctor of Ministry program was designed to assist parents of teenagers to understand and influence them as they confront and are confronted by the relativism of postmodern thinking. Her background provides her with a sensitivity and motivation to accurately confront today's culture.

Her writing skills enable her to tell her story clearly and forcefully. With great experience as an author and editor, she does an excellent job of telling her story.

I plan to use this book and recommend it to others in the ministry of reaching and teaching.

—KENNETH MAYTON, ED. D.

Assistant Dean for Doctoral Studies

Oral Roberts University School of Theology and Missions

ACKNOWLEDGMENTS

THERE ARE NUMEROUS PEOPLE who helped both inspire and equip me for the ministry to which I have been called—and the writing of this book. Besides those named on the Dedication page, I would also like to acknowledge these people:

My sister, Carolyn Holliday, whose profound, godly wisdom and words of assurance of Jesus' love for me touched me in many a dark hour of my search. Her help to me has been priceless.

Carolyn's husband, (Pastor) Phil Holliday, whose Christlike love and mentorship to Terry and me has been priceless, as well.

Joy Strang, who has inspired me that writing can be a powerful ministry to others.

Ruth Lopez Whitfield, whose leadership in the writing of my "Power Up" columns has helped me share with others the daily insights of the things of God.

Brenda J. Davis (of *SpiritLed Woman* magazine), whose godly editorial direction (in my writing for that magazine) has helped me to grow and develop as a "writing minister."

Professors, Dr. Kenneth Mayton and Dr. Paul L. King—both of Oral Roberts University—who have taught, inspired, and equipped me for my ministry calling.

Gerry Farrow Werber, Administrative Assistant to Kenneth Mayton (in the Department of Doctoral Studies), who has spoken encouragement and hope into my life, as I pursued my studies in seminary.

The editorial team at Strang Communications—Dr. Allen Quain, for his wisdom and guidance on my book, and to Robert Caggiano and Virginia Maxwell, whose valuable insights and professional expertise helped shape my book.

Atalie Anderson, Acquisitions Editor of Creation House, whose wisdom and help gave me direction in how to "make it all happen."

To all, I say, "Thank you! I could not have done this book without you!"

And above all, to my Lord and Savior Jesus Christ—*without* whom I am nothing, and *with* whom I am blessed. I am so thankful for what You did for me on the cross, enabling me to transform into a new creature, moving from New Age to *new life* in You!

INTRODUCTION

∼

IN A GRADUATE-LEVEL COLLEGE class on religious cults where I lectured recently, I was astounded to find nearly 80 percent of the students—these were grown people at least thirty years of age—had parents who were currently lost in occult practices. They told me that some of their parents were using psychic abilities or doing horoscopes. While others were espousing views that either came against Christ, or ignored Him altogether, many were seeking new wisdom and enlightenment. Disturbed by the news of it all, I was reminded of God's Word:

> This wisdom does not descend from above, but is earthly, sensual, demonic.
> —JAMES 3:15, NKJV

I was also reminded of a moment in my life—where my own dark past appeared to catch up with me.

Embarrassing Moment

My husband Terry and I were applying for passports at the post office, when I came face-to-face with something ugly on line five of our marriage license—my former identity and occupation as Sandra McNeil, *professional psychic*.

My mind raced. *What would the passport official think? What if I was denied a passport?*

Terry spoke, breaking through my dread, "Honey, maybe that word *psychic* is there for a reason." Before I could argue, he added, "It's a testimony—'Look what the Lord has done!'" In that moment, memories from my New Age and occult past overtook the present, reminding me of how I became a psychic.

Free now in Christ!

Now when I recall the incident of line five, I am reminded that regardless of my past, my future is now *free in Christ*! I am no longer a practicing psychic, but a practicing ordained minister of the gospel. I now have another history. It is one of six years of completing my graduate degrees in ministry. But more important, I now have a hope and a future for all of eternity in Christ Jesus.

This is a book of one woman's journey from the occult and New Age beliefs to *new life in Christ*. It is a book of how I fell into it, what I did in it—and what it did to me—and how through Christ I found my way out. Whether or not you believe that psychics are real is not the point of this book. Obviously there is ongoing appeal for such things or God's Word would not keep warning against them. The point of my book is to show triumph over sin and darkness and to show how the very hand of God delivered one woman from the seductive grip of Satan.

As a minister I have discovered there are many people walking among us who are lost in the darkness of the occult and New Age and do not know it. Like a rapidly spreading cancer, the occult/New Age is making its way into daily life through the broadcast media, books, business, and yes, even the church. Its influences are so widespread and disturbingly subtle that it is difficult to tell what they are, where they are, and what they are promoting.

I have included in this book distinct scenes, like snapshots from a trip, followed by reflections in which I look back on experiences or thoughts about the scenes with theological and biblical perspectives. I address issues of how to help loved ones lost in the occult/New Age, but the advice is applicable to friends, coworkers, and strangers. Hopefully, any help offered will give the reader more insight into the darkness of which I write and how to combat it and move out from under it, whether that would be for the reader or their loved ones and others. My journey is a path from darkness to the light of Christ. It is offered with love and points to the unconditional

love of our Lord and Savior Jesus Christ, who desires that
we all walk free in Him.

Sections of this book

Chapters 2 through 9 have five significant parts:

1. MY JOURNEY: In the first section I share
   what happened to me during my journey into,
   through, and eventually out of the occult/New
   Age.

2. REFLECTIONS: In this second section, I look
   back at the events shared and give insights as
   well as ministerial viewpoints. With that are
   biblical direction and theological reasoning as
   to what was happening.

3. WHAT CAN BE DONE? In this third section
   are practical applications for anyone desiring
   to point the way to Christ for those lost in the
   occult/New Age or others simply confused by
   the relativism of the culture in which we live.

4. PRAYER STRATEGIES: In this fourth
   section are suggestions for strategies with which
   to pray for the lost, especially those lost in the
   occult/New Age.

5. TALKING IT OVER: The fifth section poses valuable questions either for the reader alone to ponder, or for groups in the church, seminary, or university to discuss in an "iron-sharpening-iron" approach. (See Proverbs 27:17.)

As a special help to the reader, chapter 10 offers prayers presented as models to pray.

For whom this book is written

I have written this book for anyone seeking to know more about the occult and the New Age, whether it be the layperson, the pastor for ministerial purposes, the church leader who would like to lead groups, or the university or seminary professor who would like to inform and help train ministers to minister Christ to the lost.

It is my hope that *From New Age to New Life* will present help, inspiration, and ministry to those reading it. It is my prayer that it will point to the transforming power of Jesus Christ that is far greater than the darkness of a culture that so often denies Him.

CHAPTER 1

~

WHERE IS JESUS?

And besides all this, between us and you there
is a great gulf fixed, so that those who want to
pass from here to you cannot, nor can those from
there pass to us.

—Luke 16:26

I READ THE LETTER that had just arrived in the mail. It
was from my two aunts in Kansas, Bernice Holden and
Nellie Bacon.

I had just sent them a full-page clipping of an article
written about my psychic accomplishments. Eager for
their support, I ripped open the envelope. What met my
eyes was a surprise. Instead of being impressed with the
article, they first told me how much they loved me. And

second, with even more force, they expressed concern that I had strayed from my Christian faith.

Aunt Bernice went on to ask, "Sandra, where is Jesus?"

This question caused me to wonder, "Who was Aunt Bernice to ask me such a question in light of all my success as a celebrity psychic?" It also caused me to begin questioning, "Who am *I*?" and, "Where had Jesus been all these years since my youth?"

A simple question such as this was the beginning of a journey that would take me from the depths of darkness to the light of Christ's redemption and salvation.

∼

CHAPTER 2

WHERE DO THEY COME FROM?

Before I formed you in the womb I knew you.

—JEREMIAH 1:5

MY JOURNEY

WHERE DO OCCULTISTS AND psychics come from? My journey of life began at the end of World War II. During the war, Mother and I lived with Daddy's parents, Grandma and Grandpa Sparks, in their big house in Topeka, Kansas, where my two aunts and an uncle also lived. Grandpa would gather the family at night and read from the big family Bible. When I was three, Mother knelt at the side of my bed and I said prayers for Daddy, who was in the service in the war against Japan. When Daddy came home after the war, we moved just outside of Topeka and visited Grandma and Grandpa Sparks several times a week.

Mother said that my first words were in prayer. One night as she prayed that the Lord would bring Daddy home, I broke in with, "Home Daddy! Home Daddy, Home!" Months later, Daddy came home. I knelt at his feet for several minutes and declared, "Daddy? Home?" A little girl saw before her very eyes that God answered her prayers.

Grandpa and Grandma

Grandpa worked for the railroad and was from a long family line of strong believers, among whom was William Jennings Bryan. He loved Jesus and daily spoke of His love for me. I remember Grandpa's prayers at the Sunday dinner table. They were long enough to cool the hottest of meals. Grandma let him know it with a swift kick under the table.

Grandma loved Jesus too. Grandma also loved bingo. Once a year, limited to one day only, at the Topeka fair, Grandma would combine her zeal for both Jesus and bingo in the fairgrounds bingo tent: "C'mon, Jesus! Give Grandma B9!"

Daddy

When it came to praising the Lord, Daddy often sang the Lord's Prayer at night in his lounge chair. As Daddy sang, I felt a special warmth and presence flood the room—the same kind when Grandpa spoke of Jesus.

Daddy worked for the Santa Fe railroad and traveled during the week. When he was home on the weekends, he and Mother worked at planting a church in Pauline, Kansas. Daddy led the praise and worship part of the church service. He had such a beautiful voice that when he opened the service in song, it was as if the angels of heaven were gliding into the sanctuary singing along with him.

In Brother Lawrence's book, *The Practice of the Presence of God*, he stated, "Nothing can give us so great relief in the trials and sorrows of life as a loving relationship with God."[1] My early exposure to Daddy worshiping the Lord in song gave me a memory that would one day help me to reconnect with the roots of my Christian faith after seasons lost in hell.

My world rocked

My daddy died on my thirteenth birthday. I was awakened by a loud, pained moan from somewhere in the house. It was the sound of someone calling out in great pain. Downstairs my daddy was having a heart attack. Before I could scramble out of bed to race downstairs, the most incredible blue light in the form of an angel stopped me. I had never seen an angel before, but I knew that he was there to take Daddy to Jesus.

We all sang the Lord's Prayer at Daddy's funeral. The presence of the Lord was surely in that place. As I viewed Daddy's lifeless body in the casket, I could hear from somewhere afar his voice singing the Lord's Prayer with a chorus of angels. I am convinced that this was a special gift to me from a merciful and loving God to let a sad little girl know her Daddy was now in heaven! Grandpa taught me all about heaven through God's Word. The angel in the room made it easy to believe.

TEEN YEARS: THE LORD'S PRESENCE

Speaking of angels, I was far from being one in the years to follow. Mother, my two sisters, and I settled in the small town of Emporia, Kansas. Although I felt the Lord's love in this season, it was just plain hard without a daddy, so I did not behave well in class.

At school

I was a whisperer, a note passer, and a wise cracker. As a result, I became a regular member of detention hall. Actually, I got kicked out of there, too! One day the teacher, Coach Pike, who was in charge of detention hall, asked the group if we had any suggestions about how to make it a more effective place. I do not know what came over me, but I found myself offering him this advice: "You know, you could make this a more *appealing* place if you served cookies and punch!"

The teacher, a war veteran with a metal plate in his forehead, lowered his head. This was not a good sign! To the detention hall regulars it meant that the teacher's forehead was about to throb, flashing red-white-red. Then came the deepest voice I had ever heard, "Sparks, that's it! Leave now! Now! And take the rest of these rebels with you!" The detention hall gang, as we were often called, cleared the room before the voice got any lower. I looked back to see that the forehead was still flashing white–red.

At the ping-pong table

The next day Coach Pike caught me chewing gum and passing notes. He spoke to me after class and surprised me with words of sympathy about Daddy's death. He also surprised me with an invitation to join the girl's ping-pong team. Savvy enough to know that this might be my ticket to a better grade in his math class, I signed on. I was soon beating every kid in the school during lunch hours. My victories made me feel good. It also felt good to make it to the finals. No longer did I have a need to chew gum, whisper, or misbehave in class.

J. Robert Clinton's book, *The Making of a Leader*, related clearly how God brings us to new levels in our lives through people and circumstances.[2] This season of the coach did just that. No longer did I act up in class; after all, I operated on a new level of self-esteem. I was on Coach Pike's winning ping-pong team.

At church

Beside ping-pong, the Sunday night youth group at the church became a focal point of fellowship throughout high school. My Sunday night youth group became a way of life. Our small group of ten—six robust girls and four shy, scrawny boys—met for supervised field trips to the park, the museum, the ice cream shop, and then to volunteer for Saturday fundraisers such as bake sales in front of grocery stores, car washes, and rummage sales.

A. B. Bruce reminds us in his book, *The Training of the Twelve*, that as believers we are to set ourselves apart as disciples.[3] The coach and the church youth fellowship set me apart in those days to a lifestyle that avoided the drugs and wild behavior other kids experienced.

REFLECTIONS

LOOKING BACK THROUGH THE eyes of experience, I see that I was raised in a "good Christian home." I also see how "good kids" can fall into "bad" at any age, regardless of how good of a Christian home they were raised in. Why? We live in a fallen world in an age when other worldviews and beliefs conflict with Christian beliefs. In my case, as I will share in the next chapter, I wound up overtaken and overpowered by beliefs and influences that countered Christ.

WHAT CAN BE DONE?

IS THERE ANYTHING THAT can be done to prevent your loved ones from being drawn to the beliefs and influences that oppose Christ and the Christian walk? Parents, the seeds you have sown into your child, whether or not he or she is actively serving the Lord, are *not* lost, even if your child grows up and loses their way. I know, because that is what happened to me. Spouses, the investment of time and faith you have made in prayer for your husband or wife who is cut off from the Lord is *not* for naught.

The lost are not lost by choice!

The Lord is faithful and merciful. He will honor your faith that your loved ones influenced by the occult/ New Age will be saved and will serve Him! Jesus said in Matthew 9:29, "According to your faith be it unto you" (KJV). The word *unto* in Greek is a preposition that connotes a passage or a system of delivery. When you and I have faith, regardless of the circumstances, our faith is like a passage or system of delivery through which the Lord can deliver or bring "unto" us the answers to our prayers. This is not "name it and claim it," which really does not involve prayer but rather snappy orders. This is receiving what the Lord already has for us after we have asked Him. So press on in your faith that your loved ones will be set free from occult/New Age influences and take up a strong position in Christ!

PRAYER STRATEGIES

A PERSON IS NEVER so lost as to not need or be able to benefit from our prayers. The Lord is never too far from any person in need to hear prayers for him or her. No situation is ever so far beyond the Father's hand that it cannot be helped or changed by prayer.

Your strategy is to pray, pray, and pray for your loved ones, friends, business associates, and even strangers! And do it with God's love and compassion for the lost! Remember, the lost are often not lost by choice!

TALKING IT OVER

HERE ARE SOME QUESTIONS that might be explored and discussed between you the reader and your friends, among members of the church in a more formal setting, or among pupils in a seminary setting. These hypothetical questions can be delved into—knowing that each person might have his or her varying perspective—in an "iron-sharpening-iron" climate:

1. In what ways might parents today influence their children to be stronger in the Lord against the evils and antichrist influences of the age?

2. Discuss the definition of the term *disciple* and how we can be disciples of Christ in our various day-to-day situations.

CHAPTER 3

~

WHAT'S A NICE GIRL LIKE YOU DOING IN A PLACE LIKE THIS?

But the cowardly, unbelieving, abominable, murderers, sexually immoral, sorcerers, idolaters, and all liars shall have their part in the lake which burns with fire and brimstone, which is the second death.

—REVELATION 21:8

MY JOURNEY

AFTER HIGH SCHOOL I attended college in my hometown of Emporia, Kansas, then married and went to California to teach. After five years of unhappiness over mental abuse, I divorced my husband. I do not talk about it now, because I have forgiven him, and it is all under the blood of Jesus.

During those years of our marriage I became increasingly isolated. I grew distant from my parents and sisters and friends. I stopped going to church and talking to the Lord.

Hello, Hollywood!

After the divorce I moved to Hollywood where it was easy to drift into being whatever I wanted to be. It was the 1970s when "do your own thing" and "be your own best friend" were the standards of the day. I thought I could be free to step away from anything I had ever been and become a brand new being—by my standards and not God's. But I had a problem. I was no longer a wife. I did not have a church. I was now living in a bleak one-room apartment and struggling financially. I knew I wanted to be "somebody"—but *whom*? I felt needy and helpless; I felt like a failure. "Why would God do this to me?" I thought. "Where has He been? What did I do to deserve this?"

Reeling from the divorce and needing guidance, I went to a counseling session with a secular psychologist in Beverly Hills. During my hour in his office, I opened up and admitted that my sensitivity was hurting me. I felt alone. I felt angry about my divorce. I felt hurt by the attitudes of our former friends who ditched me because we were no longer a couple.

I sat there on the couch, eyes closed, pouring out my heart about how sad I was about everything—the divorce, my life, and my being too sensitive for my own good. I went into great detail. Why, I could even feel what people all around me were feeling! *What was wrong with me?*

When I opened my eyes, I saw not the face of an interested psychologist, but the distracted face that was focused on—his mistress! This was something I just "knew"—I don't know how and I don't know why! But I suddenly knew that this joker was sitting there, taking my hard-earned money, pretending to care about my story, yet was really counting down the minutes until he could meet his mistress for lunch. What did I do? I stood up and said, "This is enough! You can go have lunch with her now!" I paid my bill at the front desk and walked out, sure that I would never hear from this guy. Was I ever wrong! Late that night, I received a call from a phone booth. I recognized the therapist's voice, "Uh, Sandra. McNeil? I'm sorry about today. By the way, there are people who might be able to use you and your, uh, special talents."

Welcome to the lab

The psychologist put me in touch with a group at a local university, which was testing volunteers for "psychic abilities"—as I was told, "Under a Defense Department grant." The university department of psychology was involved with testing people on their "mind power abilities," to see if they could "see or sense things at a distance," along with other extrasensory abilities. This was the first time in my life that I encountered the term *psychic* and certainly the first moment in my life when I was told I might have such abilities!

I reported to the university lab where I was tested for my psychic abilities. I was given a letter to hold and was asked by a professor to describe in detail the person who had written it to her. I was asked to describe that person's physical features, temperament, emotions at the time of writing, and what the contents of the letter might be. This was called an experiment in telemetry or fingering an object and getting sensations from it. This was an unofficial test, but was a determining factor in my selection for more experiments on psychic abilities.

When I returned home I was welcomed by the flashing red light on my answering machine. It was the professor. I was invited to take part in more experiments. The professor said that I had done very well and that I would be a good subject. This made me smile. It felt good to be called good, and I was pleased to know that I was needed, even if it was for lab experiments.

Every Tuesday I reported to the lab and entered a booth where I was tested on such things as mental telepathy (tapping into the thoughts of others), ESP (sensing things about people and objects without any information given to me), and remote viewing (viewing in my "mind's eye" locations, people, and events). I was generally accurate, but I was most accurate in picking up on emotions of those in the next booths. At times the technicians would become quite frustrated with me, because there were no instruments capable of measuring what I was getting!

Missing persons

Needing to be needed, I became a human guinea pig, reporting to the university lab once a week. There, I took part in a variety of tests for psychic abilities, including work on missing persons' cases. When I arrived, there would be a bag that was tagged with a typed note of the missing person's case. I was provided a tape recorder into which I recorded my impression of the person, his or her life, and what happened to them. I used remote viewing as a technique to find out locations. At times it worked, while at other times it didn't. Little did I know that I was tapping into the occult, or hidden, demonic realms with my sensitivities, outside of God's help. If only I had read His Word that warns us against this practice:

> There shall not be found among you anyone who...practices witchcraft, or a soothsayer, or one who interprets omens, or a sorcerer, or one who conjures spells, or a medium, or a spiritist, or

one who calls up the dead. For all who do these things are an abomination to the LORD, and because of these abominations the LORD your God drives them out from before you.

—DEUTERONOMY 18:10–12

During this season I met a famous bounty hunter and his wife who would stop by my apartment with names of people who had jumped bail. I would "tune in" and get cities where I felt the missing persons of interest were. This was frustrating, because I began to feel as if I were tracking a hunted animal. So after three or four sessions, I stopped.

Mistaken identity at the lab

The most humorous and embarrassing incident that happened to me during my testing at the university was when a film crew from *CBS Evening News* arranged to come to do a story about psychics and Kirlian photography (photography used to capture energies off the human body). The experiments involved psychics and their abilities to pick up on those energies.

On the day of filming, I reported to the lab with my hair coiffed and my camera-ready makeup applied. As the crew set up the cameras, I excused myself from the lab and went down a hall to find a restroom.

What I did not know was that within that same building were patients being treated for mental disorders. I managed to find the ladies room, but I could not find my way back to the lab. Feeling a bit panicked, I stopped an attendant in a white uniform. "Excuse me," I said, "I'm a bit lost. I have to get back to the lab, because I am going to be on Walter Cronkite." Instead of directions, I got a sympathetic smile from someone who was used to dealing with people with overblown delusions. "How nice, dear," she responded.

Weeknight fun

I really looked forward to Thursday nights. Those were the nights when I reported to the recreation room of a tall luxury condo in Marina del Rey. The members of our little group of experiment psychics would report there to do further work on missing persons cases. These sessions involved us sitting in a friendly circle and "tuning in" on missing persons or escaped criminals or suspects on certain official cases (police or detective). If someone couldn't come up with a detail, four others would. There was no lab technician keeping score. It was more of a groupthink atmosphere, and the back table had an endless supply of cookies, coffee, and soft drinks. I always left charged up and encouraged that I had been taking part in something of value that was helping mankind.

Individual sleuthing the psychic way

It felt so good to be considered useful and needed with my psychic abilities. In that season, I began to volunteer, like other psychics, for various police cases. By day I taught high school, and after my teaching day was done, I would head for the lab once or twice a week to work on the mind experiments and to volunteer. In my mind, I was doing the world a service.

The very work that seemed to give me purpose also gave me unrest and terror!

As I tuned in with my mind's eye and let my mind view any scenes that came to me, I found that I did come up with names, faces, and locations. Success! By day, it was fun and quite addictive. The more I moved in the dimension of mind power and psychic activities of "tuning in" on people, the more I was drawn to it all. But at night, it was not so fun! When I went to bed, I often heard a tap-tap on the walls. "What was that?" There was creaking on the stairs! Was it a spirit? Or was it a figment of my imagination? Could it be the murderer of the victims I had tuned into by day? *What if I were the next victim?*

The work also made me so sad. I was sad for the victims of heinous crimes. I was growing sadder each moment for myself. I felt like a victim of my own sensitivities, trapped into seeing things that were dark, ugly, and hellish. *"Was there any way out of this?"*

One dark and stormy night

I recall one particular rainy night in my tiny apartment in Venice Beach. I was reviewing a multitude of police pictures I had arranged on the floor—pictures of young women who had been stalked, then strangled. As I fingered the photos, I attempted to see at a distance (through my inner psychic mind's sense) the face of the stalker. Just then, a crack of thunder pierced the air. With it, a shaft of light from the lightning cut through the room and lit up the photos of the dead victims' faces. They seemed to be looking up at me, mocking my attempts to find their strangler.

I felt helpless and afraid. I was alone with police photos of murder victims, and the killer was still loose! What if he had seen me pick up the photos from the door at the police station at dusk and had followed me home to my lonely apartment at the beach? He was known for stalking women who were single, alone, and cut off.

The phone's shrill ring disturbed the room. I shook from fear. Who would be calling after midnight? The voice at the other end was a police officer working on the case. Apparently the strangler was getting ready to make his strike again. The officer asked if I had managed to come up with anything yet. I told him I had not, but I promised to have something shortly. In a half hour the phone rang again. This time I *did* have something—a name and a location. No one ever said how close I was to nailing him, but the phone continued to ring at half-hour intervals throughout the rest of the night.

The dawn of a new day

I must have fallen asleep, for the next thing I knew I was waking up on the floor next to the pictures of the victims. This sent a shiver down my spine. I gathered the pictures, wrote a brief scenario of what I received from my mind's viewing the night before, and wasted no time driving to the police station to hand it all over.

Afterward, I stopped at a Denny's near Venice Beach. With a cup of coffee in my hand I realized that no matter how much "good" I was doing in helping solve crimes with my psychic abilities, it was just too nightmarish for me. I looked around and saw couples smiling over pancakes and moms with chattering kids in booths. Everyone seemed to have a life but me. My relatives were across the country. The only thing I seemed to have going for me these days were either runaways, dead people I was tracking down, or the killers who had done away with them. I had to get out of this. Could I?

Polishing off a sweet roll with one last swig of now-cold coffee, I rose from my booth. Forgetting I was in a public place, I exclaimed out loud my innermost thoughts about psychic crime work—"It's the pits!" A crowd of three at the next table paused and took a good hard look at me. The waitress jumped in with, "I'll have you know we baked our rolls this morning!" Too tired to argue or explain the misunderstanding, I paid my bill and left. I had not slept all night, and my only thought was getting home and crawling into bed. My next thought after that was, "This is the last time I'll ever deal with photos of dead bodies!"

Bride of Frankenstein

Feeling that I still needed to use my brain for the good of mankind, I volunteered (after being approached) for experiments on "alpha states and psychic levels of mind." These experiments took place at a local hospital. Again, I was an anonymous "number." The good news was that there were no runaways, dead bodies to tune in to, or macabre, unsolved police cases.

What I was to do was tune in to objects that the other subjects were holding in the next room. While I was doing this, there was equipment for taking an electroencephalogram (EEG) that measured my brain waves. The purpose was to see if psychic activity could be measured by alpha waves of the brain. No matter how "good" my cause, I still could not shake the feeling that my life was empty, and that was no way to live. "Was I no different than a rat in a cage?" I wondered.

On the night before Thanksgiving when people were traveling home to be with loved ones, I was in a dark room with my head hooked up to EEG equipment. I was doing another experiment on brain waves and psychic activity. I happened to notice my own image in the mirror, complete with white spiked hair and electrode cream oozing from beneath the EEG sensors.

"No!" I shouted at the image in the mirror. I looked like the bride of Frankenstein. "This is it! No more!"

"What's happened to you?" the lab technician snapped, racing into the room. Apparently with my outburst of anger, my brain waves had gone wild. The bride of Frankenstein was acting up!

Promising to keep it all under control, I fulfilled my time, then left, never to return. I raced to the car, not stopping to even wash off the electrode cream or to push down the spiked hair. I can imagine what people in their cars thought as I raced past them in traffic. Of course this was Los Angeles—the heart of show business and show people going to movie shoots. No doubt they thought I was speeding toward my next horror movie shoot.

Strange encounter

One day while visiting the library in my quest to get more books on the occult, I encountered a most unusual man. He was wearing a black coat and was slumped over in his chair at one of the reading tables. The table happened to be next to the occult section where I was headed to pick up more books on witchcraft, sorcery, and talking with the dead.

Just as I was about to cross beyond his chair, he sat up and spoke to me, "Young lady, stop! You are headed the wrong way. Those books will harm you, not help you. You also must get rid of the books you have at home on your coffee table."

It wasn't his statement or his knowledge of my books at home that stopped me in my tracks; it was his face. It was rather swarthy with eyes that looked like the blue of heaven. All around him was an unusual golden glow—in fluid form. "What is going on?" I asked myself.

Then the stranger asked, "Is it power you seek?" Before I could answer, he stated lovingly but firmly, "Seek the Lord your God. Pursue wisdom through God, not through the counterfeit. You'll see."

With that, the mysterious stranger bowed his head into folded arms and apparently went back to sleep. To add to the strangeness of this moment, a library worker came up to me and announced that I could not go over to that section now, because it was closed for repairs.

I walked briskly out of the library with the feeling of a force at my back. To this day, I do not know who that man was. Could he have been the Lord manifested? An angel? I do know this—I am sure now that the Lord used that man and that situation to prevent me from plummeting further into hell.

Search into hell

"Who am I?" I began to question why I wasn't fulfilled in doing activities that I was good at. After all, here I was, performing functions that were helping "the cause of research for a good purpose of seeing what the powers of mind could do." And here I was using some "talents" that I had, often doing "well" according to the researchers. So why wasn't I fulfilled or happy in all of this?

A search began mainly to find myself. So I began to read more and more about the supernatural. Little did I know that this path of personal seeking was leading me to the very depths of what looked and felt like hell. It would take a miracle of God for me to get out!

REFLECTIONS

IN REFLECTING ON THOSE days, I see where the lure of the supernatural was very appealing to me. After five years of an unhappy marriage I was free to explore the unknown and exciting powers of the mind. I was naturally ripe to be a participant in a movement focusing on the self and its powers—the New Age movement.

According to researcher Barbara Paulin, the New Age movement, born of Eastern mysticism practices, promotes the self and its own individual sensory perceptions.[1] With my psychic activities, I was an active participant in the New Age movement, whether I knew it or not.

Addicted

At the time of my involvement in psychic lab experiments and in volunteering to work on missing persons and murder cases, I became addicted to the thrill of being my own person with special powers and looking beyond what met the eye. When I tuned in I was outside the space-time continuum (just like a space traveler—a veritable star trekker). I was free to explore a vast void where future possibilities existed. This gave me a sense of wonder and worth and my own power.

WHAT CAN BE DONE?

I HAVE A NOTE of encouragement for those who have loved ones lost in the occult/New Age. Remember that they are lost, but are not lost causes. God's Word reminds us that there is no place on Earth we can go to escape or hide from Him, and that means the saved and unsaved:

> Where can I go from Your Spirit? Or where can I flee from Your presence? If I ascend into heaven, You are there; If I make my bed in hell, behold, You are there. If I take the wings of the morning, And dwell in the uttermost parts of the sea, Even there Your hand shall lead me, And Your right hand shall hold me. If I say, "Surely the darkness shall fall on me," Even the night shall be light about me; Indeed, the darkness shall not hide from You, But the night shines as the day; The darkness and the light are both alike to You.
>
> —PSALM 139:7–12

For family members lost in the occult/New Age

Just because a family member is lost in the occult/New Age does not mean that you have to separate him or her from yourself. That would be the worst thing you could do. It would only force your loved one further away from you and the Christian "camp"—and further isolate them within the camp of the enemy.

The best thing you can do is include your lost loved ones in family activities. If your loved one does not choose to come, keep inviting them. Have dinners and gatherings in the home. Sooner or later they might attend. It cannot hurt, and you have everything to gain. If they are across the country, write to them. That is what my family did. My aunts who asked, "Where is Jesus?" had a powerful impact on me even though they were far away.

Do you feel powerful enough?

Do you feel powerful enough to make a difference in the life of your lost loved one? Probably not! But it is not you who can save him or her. You and I cannot save a gnat! So perhaps we should let the Holy Spirit work on their spirits and hearts as we continue to let Jesus Christ move through us with His love—a love that is uncondi- tional and greater than any resistance that could possibly fight back.

I have learned that we as Christian witnesses must at some point step back and let the Holy Spirit do His stuff. We must make room for the unbeliever to genuinely receive Jesus without being forced. My message to anyone with a loved one lost in the occult/New Age is this: do not give up! God hasn't! Look to His promise in Psalm 139. He knows your loved ones and knows exactly where they are! *Press on in faith!* God's Word is full of encouragement to not give up! Read 2 Corinthians 4, which encourages us not to give up no matter how "hard pressed" the circumstances. (See 2 Corinthians 4:8.) Then read 2 Corinthians 5:7, "For we walk by faith, not by sight." God not only answers prayer, but He will also work a miracle on your lost loved one! Never lose sight of that.

PRAYER STRATEGIES

THE THING TO REMEMBER when praying for a lost loved one is that you are to love him or her! God's Word teaches us that there is really a principality influencing them:

> For we do not wrestle against flesh and blood, but against principalities, against powers, against the rulers of the darkness of this age, against spiritual hosts of wickedness in the heavenly places.
> —EPHESIANS 6:12

Hate the sin, not the sinner! God's Word reminds us that God is love, and we should walk in love:

> Beloved, let us love one another, for love is of God; and everyone who loves is born of God and knows God. He who does not love does not know

God, for God is love. In this the love of God was
manifested toward us, that God has sent His only
begotten Son into the world, that we might live
through Him.

—1 John 4:7–9

When we attempt to minister Jesus to our loved
ones—whether through acts of including them in our
activities or through speaking of Him—we must do it in
love. If the loved one appears too lost or closed to what we
do or say with the love of the Lord in us, our efforts are
never for naught! They are seeds planted through our
"seed faith" that the Lord will take our efforts and honor
them as seed that will grow over time.

What to pray for

The key is to pray in one of two ways. Pray *against*
the holds that keep them bound (the principalities), or *for*
the loved one to receive the Lord. In either case, it is good
to pray and agree with someone else that your prayers be
answered, according to the Lord's promise to be there
with you:

If two of you agree on earth concerning anything that they ask, it will be done for them by
My Father in heaven. For where two or three are

gathered in My name, I am there in the midst
of them.

—MATTHEW 18:19–20

TALKING IT OVER

1. Discuss ways in which it is easy for people of any
   age to be drawn into the occult/New Age.

2. Discuss why young people are drawn to the
   occult/New Age.

3. Discuss why the occult/New Age is not
   innocent.

~

CHAPTER 4

PULL OF THE DARK VORTEX

For everyone practicing evil hates the light and does not come to the light, lest his deeds should be exposed.

—JOHN 3:20

MY JOURNEY

IN MY QUEST FOR truth that could validate my "gifts" of sensing things as a psychic, I began a search that led me through doors into dark places. These places were seductive with the promise of peacefulness, where no one could hurt me; and power, where I could call the shots over my life. I did not realize that in these dark places, I was fair game for demons, incarnate spirits, and Satan himself.

Spooky things and haunted houses

One of the activities in which I found myself participating was "haunted house calls." This new activity came through the group of psychics with whom I had participated in the research at the university. A professor at the university was doing a study on haunted houses to investigate their authenticity. He also was investigating psychics to see if they could sense accurately the presence of incarnate spirits or ghosts.

Although this was another form of a psychic experiment, I felt less a rat in a cage and more of a human with a purpose involved in vital—and exciting—research. I was needed! Once a week I joined the other psychics from the university out on a haunted house call. Most of the calls were to large mansions. We were all supervised under a lead psychic. The professor conducting the research was also there taking notes.

On one particular call to a large three-story mansion, we were all instructed to spread out and walk alone down dark passageways and into vacant rooms. This was spooky to me, but what happened next began to really unhinge me.

As I stepped inside what looked like a child's room, complete with dolls and clown toys staring back at me,

I was stopped in my tracks by a sound. It was the cry of a small child. *Was this the spirit of a child who had died?* Next, without warning, my arms were in pain. Something invisible was biting them! I tried to scream, but no sound came out! I began to make my way out of the room, but my feet—feeling weighed down—could not move fast enough. I felt like I was in a nightmare where I was running from something horrible but could not move fast enough to get to safety.

Moments later, after we all assembled downstairs to share what happened, the most horrid stench rose up before all of us. There appeared in front of us all a dark, twisted figure of a man! This was full flesh and not vapor. It smelled like something that had died. We all screamed. The professor dropped his pen and passed out, falling back onto the hardwood floor!

The session ended abruptly. As we made our way to our cars, the leader of our group could not start his car. I gave him a lift to the nearest gas station. As I drove, the door on his side kept swinging wide open with the same death stench invading my car! Despite his greatest efforts to lock the door, the lock kept popping up, and the door kept swinging wide open! "It is following you home," he said matter-of-factly. At that moment I became aware of how real demons are!

After I dropped off my passenger at the gas station I drove home relieved to be away from the craziness of the haunted house. What awaited me was not an evening of peace and safety, but a nightmare—a living nightmare. There was a tapping on my bedroom walls during the night, the same stench of a dead body filled my entire apartment, and a voice from somewhere around me called, "Sa-a-a-n-d-r-a-a-a." That was the last haunted house call I ever made.

I mentioned the noises and stench to my neighbor, Carol, who had an acquaintance who was a minister. He came over and prayed, and it left. I do not know whether Carol mentioned to the minister all that I was into, but I do know that after he prayed, the manifestations left and never returned.

Conjuring up the dead

I went from investigating haunted houses to taking part in séances, sessions where groups meet around a table and try to conjure up the dead and receive messages.

A woman once asked me, "Now why would you do that?" Remember, I was still lost and searching. I was so lost that I did not associate haunted houses with what happens at séances. In my searching state, I was on a quest for answers to the questions, "Who am I?" "What special gifts do I have?" and "Can I possibly speak and interact with the dead?" Being lost I did not consult God's Word. Rather, I kept reading books on the occult and how to apply my special gifts.

My search for answers brought me to séances, usually in the context of doing it for publicity. By now, I was writing psychic predictions for a well-known tabloid magazine. A tabloid newspaper flew me to Florida to be in a séance for a famous (but dead) celebrity. At that time when I sought to have my gifts validated, this was a chance to do something unique with my gifts. I thought that this validated me further as a psychic who had special powers. Little did I know the evil in which I became involved.

I sat around tables in dark rooms and invited spirits of the dead to communicate and possibly enter someone's body in order to speak. I realize now that I was inviting evil to come and dwell in me. I shudder as I look back on that time in my life. We could have unknowingly had an evil spirit imitating someone's dear Uncle Joe. Even if we are conjuring up "dear Uncle Joe," it is still an evil practice. God has warned us in the Bible to refrain from such evil practices:

> And when they say to you, "Seek those who are mediums and wizards, who whisper and mutter," should not a people seek their God? Should they seek the dead on behalf of the living? To the law and to the testimony! If they do not speak according to this word, it is because there is no light in them.
> —ISAIAH 8:19–20

Why should we want to open ourselves to any evil thing?

On that trip to Florida, "something" followed me back to the hotel where I was staying. It was very similar to my haunted house call experience. I was spooked to wake up to find smear marks of some kind on the walls and voices around me screaming, "Help me!" This time there was no priest to help me. The only help around me was a witch who took part in the séance. She said, "I can give you special powers to take care of that." Something deep inside me made me so uneasy about her and her offer that I retreated from her all the time I was there. When I got back to my room I opened the drawer to find a Gideons Society Bible. I didn't read it, but I opened it and found myself crying out to God to protect me. In a few minutes I drifted into a deep sleep. When I awakened, the stench, the fear, and the voices were gone.

I did not know it at the time, but God was at work, moving me closer to the light of Jesus Christ!

When I got back home to Los Angeles I was aware that I had come to know a dark side of life—a pit where evil existed—through my involvement in haunted house calls and séances. I knew that I must avoid them at all costs! The sessions were scary, but what followed was always more terrifying: ghostly forms, taps on the walls, and voices haunting me in my very apartment.

Soon I was aware of something equally scary. As I began to do radio and TV shows as a psychic, I began to stir up jealousy among members of satanic churches who also wanted to be on those shows. I was picked over them, so they became angry and left messages on my phone that they were out to put a stop to me. One particular night my head felt pressured as if in a vise. I knew I was being spoken against with curses and spells from a group of members from the satanic church that phoned me with a message. I could not rest or think. In this hideous state of attack, I found myself crying out to God, "Help!" In an instant my bedroom lit up whiter and brighter than any strobe light. The light overtook the dark, and I was aware of a powerful God who was making Himself known to me in my state of satanic attack.

REFLECTIONS

I HAVE LOOKED BACK on those times and wondered, "Why didn't I just come to Jesus if things were all that dark and scary?" It was not that easy. For one thing, I was in the midst of dark and scary things and was not ready to leave them. The research was titillating. The unknown was seductive. Because I was known as a "psychic sensitive," I was needed. I felt special. Because I was so entrenched in evil, I was bound to it. I was not ready to go to Jesus and receive Him.

Choices

Over the years, after study in seminary and reading God's Word, I have come to understand the gift of choice that God has given to you and me. He did not send His Son to die on the cross *to force* us into heaven. Rather, it is up to us *to make a choice* to receive Jesus as our Savior. When Jesus sent His disciples out to make more disciples, He did not tell them to force anyone, but to "make," which involves a process. That can only come from choice. (See Matthew 28:19.)

If God could have "zapped" me into Jesus' arms that night when I was attacked at the haunted house or by the members of Satan's church, it would have been *Him forcing* me and not *me receiving* Jesus. Forcing me to Jesus would not have been God's love in action offering me a Savior.

WHAT CAN BE DONE?

WE LIVE IN A culture that appears to be anything but God fearing. Many people have become dulled and apathetic to sin. The individual today is not unlike individuals in the Book of Judges: "In those days there was no king in Israel; everyone did what was right in his own eyes" (Judg. 21:25).

In our postmodern culture, absolute truth is no longer promoted. How did we get here? According to academic researcher Russell Alexander Morris, the years 1500 to 1960 contained a cultural climate throughout the world that was more ordered and encouraged absolutes. It was referred to as the Modern Age. Since that time, there has been a cultural shift toward relativism. Morris has revealed through his research a historical pattern, where the philosophical roots of postmodernism began to form as far back as the days of Friedrich Nietzsche (1844–1900). It was Nietzsche who promoted the idea that "all we have is interpretations."[1]

In his national surveys, researcher George Barna has found that relativism has become the prevalent trait of our more liberal postmodern culture. Kids are being raised now in a climate where truth is portrayed as relative to the situation rather than being absolute where "right is right, wrong is wrong."[2] What can be done by the Christian believer to point people to the absolute truths of God in such a culture of varying worldviews?

Lines blurred

The late Francis Schaeffer, a noted theologian, explored the problem of what happens in a culture where other worldviews collide with Christian beliefs. In his book, *The God Who Is There*, he speaks of how, in such a culture with conflicting worldviews, there is bound to be a merging of languages and speech patterns that result in contrasting religions or beliefs sharing the same phrases and words, yet with those words meaning entirely different thoughts and concepts.[3] For example, the word *blessed* means blessed of one sovereign God to the Christian, but to the witch it will *not* mean blessed of one sovereign God. The name *Christ* is shared by different belief systems. I know this from experience. When I was involved with New Age, psychics, and practitioners of the occult, many used the name *Christ*—but in reference to an amorphous, cosmic being, not the risen Savior.

As believers, we must discern and listen to the words people use and what words we might use to minister to them. This will help us avoid the trap of following a cult leader and thinking he or she is a Christian.

When ministering to others, we must first discern where they are spiritually. This will enable us to reach them in ways most effective, always with love, as Frances Schaeffer reminds us, "This man is our counterpart; he is lost, but so once were we."[4]

Guess who's talking

What harm is the relativistic view of life doing to the Christian? According to one prominent pastor, such views focusing on truth being entirely relative are blurring our very distinction between good and evil.[5]

According to scholar Kevin J. Vanhoozer, our postmodern relativistic culture is an expression of antipathy toward any broad, overarching narrative—or metanarrative—or absolute truth that might explain or define life itself.[6] Since our culture is increasingly relativistic, there is a blurring of the Christian faith itself, where, if we are not careful, Jesus Christ can be exchanged for a worldview of the "state" that shuts Him off from daily life.[7] As a result, when Christian kids attend school during the week or when Christian adults go to the workplace, they are pressured to operate in a mind-set that is not only Christ-less, but in some cases outright antichrist. Theologian James Sire, in his book, *Why Good Arguments Often Fail*, has cited a study:

> …of the religious and spiritual lives of American teenagers. [Where] sociologists Christian Smith and Melinda Lundquist Denton analyze the results of in-depth interviews of 267 teenagers and conclude that religious relativism is the pervasive background assumptions of most teens who identify themselves as Christian.[8]

In this same study, one teen was saying of another (with a conflicting opinion): "I couldn't say anything. It's their opinion. I have my own opinion."⁹ As Smith and Denton have commented in the study:

> When each individual has his or her own unique and self-authenticating experiences and felt needs and desires, it is impossible for any (alien) individual to properly evaluate or judge those chosen beliefs, commitments, desires, or lifestyles. The typical bywords, rather, are "Who am I to judge?" "If that's what they choose, whatever." "Each person decides for himself," and "If it works for them, fine.¹⁰

As one who was greatly influenced by New Age practices within our open-minded and liberal postmodern culture, I felt free to explore and to search. Was that such a bad thing? No! But the bad thing was I searched in all the wrong places. In a culture without borders of right and wrong there is that risk that people will get lost in belief systems that are counter Christ.

Researcher and theologian Leonard Sweet has asserted that we must not turn our backs, however, on the postmodern culture, but rather work with it. For instance, in our churches we can work with ways of communicating (e-mails, language styles) that the people can understand, thereby reaching them.¹¹

As a former psychic, I have counseled many who are

coming away from New Age activities (such as forms of the occult and psychic dabblings) into the church. I am seeing that New Agers need to be discipled and transitioned into the church in encouraging ways. This can only be done, as Leonard Sweet suggests, if the church works with them, using language that is meaningful to them.

Parents can be better equipped to guide and mentor their teens away from the evils of the age. In my doctor of ministry applied research project, *Equipping Parents Who Have Teens Influenced by the Relativism of a Postmodern Culture*, I have written of these concerns, namely how to equip parents to minister Christlike values to their teens in a culture that either minimizes Him, ignores Him, or hates Him.[12] The results of my study have shown that parents can indeed be equipped to effectively minister to teens the absolute values of Christian beliefs.[13]

PRAYER STRATEGIES

IF YOU HAVE A loved one or know someone who is deeply involved in the occult or New Age, the best thing you can do is let him or her be transformed in a process rather than forcing them to repent. It is, after all, the Holy Spirit who will convict their hearts and draw them to a Savior. You can merely point the way. The most effective way to do that is through love.

TALKING IT OVER

1. Discuss books that might be given to those practicing the occult. Choose books that can be used as ministry tools to point the way to Jesus Christ. If you are in a group setting, discuss why these books might be effective ministry tools.

2. Discuss ways in which you might encourage a lost loved one to get to church without condemning or forcing.

3. Discuss the pull of the dark—the occult—and Christ-centered alternatives to pull teens and adults away from it all.

CHAPTER 5

~

CAN YOU DO IT
TO DRUMS?

I have not come to call the righteous, but sinners,
to repentance.

—LUKE 5:32

MY JOURNEY

THE SEASON OF PSYCHIC experiments led me to go
public. As I was living in Los Angeles, the media and
promotions capital of the world, I naturally got invited
to do media. A promotions group for a popular cruise
line invited me to do a psychic floor show in the lounge
of a well-known cruise ship. When I met with them, the
director looked over his reading glasses, then asked, "Hey!

53

Can you do it to drums in a low-cut dress?" As fast as I
answered, "No!" I was out the door.

What? Quit show biz?

Doing talk shows appealed to me, so I accepted a daily
live spot on a popular radio station in the L.A. suburb of
Northridge. My morning live spot advised the audience of
mostly housewives about its day ahead and how to make
it a positive and prosperous one. Soon I became known as
"the prosperity psychic." One day as I was phoning in my
one-minute live report from a phone booth on the corner
of Venice Beach, another voice broke in over mine, "This
is the operator. Your time has expired. Please insert twen-
ty-five cents to continue." Since I did not have a quarter to
rub between my two fingers, I was cut off…live! Good-
bye prosperity psychic!

It's showtime!

In my season of going public I became a regular personality not just in Los Angeles, but also in New York
on the morning shows. Regis Philbin was the host of the
A.M. Los Angeles show, so when I was his guest every two
weeks, I would advise him and callers (calling in live) of
their week ahead, helping them all with their concerns.

On one live audience show from New York, a woman
with a distinct Brooklyn accent and a smoky voice
called in. "Do you see a man in my fute-cha?" she asked,

reminding me of the late Selma Diamond. I did see a man in her future—or "fute-cha." I bravely declared that within the next two weeks she might be meeting him. Unfortunately, two weeks later, while doing the live call-ins, I was met with the same smoky voice, "So where *is* he?" It turns out this woman had never left the house, waiting on Mr. Perfect to come into her life!

During that same season, I was hired (as Sandra McNeil) to be a principle performer on a national TV series in Canada on the CBC network. The series was called *Beyond Reason.* Some people from CBC had seen me on the ABC shows and decided that I would be good for the *Beyond Reason* show, which was already a hit game show. I went to Toronto, Canada, for three weeks and taped the series.

Showstoppers and scene-stealers

In my season of going public, I was exposed to other psychics going public. While I did meet some authentic ones, I also met a lot of fake ones. These were the show-stoppers, or scene-stealers. They knew how to make a dramatic show of it. They made it look like they were getting the scoop on people, when all the while they were using tricks. They were no different from magicians using sleight-of-hand tricks. One trick, shared with me by a well-known psychic, was to get the person's nationality and to pick a name common to it. Then the trick was to make it seem as if the psychic were "picking up on" a name from the ether. "Honey," she confided, "I have advice for you! If you want people to think you are accurate, first get their nationality. If they are Italian, tell them you sense there is a Tony. Tony's a common Italian name. Who doesn't have a Tony—dead or alive—in the family tree? You can't lose!"

I might have been lost in the occult/New Age, but I wasn't a con artist! *This* advice I did not take to the bank!

Behind the scenes

I soon met Terry, who was the sweetest, most precious (and handsome) man! As the associate producer of *A.M. Los Angeles, Live with Regis Philbin*, Terry Clifton booked me as the show's regular psychic. It turned out that Terry too was lost in New Age—not as a practitioner, but as someone interested in it and unchurched.

Terry and I would have breakfast in the ABC commissary after the show. More often than not, our conversation drifted to how we (unlike other people) were never going to get married! I look back and see not only the Lord's hand, but that He must have been smiling and saying, "Oh really, Sandra?" After nearly a year of discussion about why were never going to get married, Terry and I got married in a New Age church.

Damascus road on the platform

As I became more known as a psychic/TV personality, I was invited to more speaking engagements on the powers of the mind. Often I was invited as a motivational speaker to speak to large conventions of bankers and medical people interested in utilizing the powers of the mind.

It was during this time that I sent a big press clipping to my two aunts in Kansas and got back the startling question, "Sandra, where is Jesus?" Although I hated to admit it, that question seemed to be like a thorn in my side daily. The more I pressed forward as a practicing celebrity psychic and motivational speaker, the more Aunt Bernice and Aunt Nellie's letter pressed into my mind!

One evening just a few months after Terry and I were married, I was on the auditorium platform about to begin my motivational powers-of-the-mind speech to a convention of two thousand bankers. I took my place at the podium and faced the crowd (of what appeared to be a sea of men in white socks). I began the teaser, "Do you know how powerful you are?"

No sooner than I had thrown forth my pitch to the crowd of bankers, I heard a voice on all sides of me. There, in front of God and everyone, I knew that I was hearing the voice of the Lord, "Do you know how powerful I am, Sandra?"

Stopped in my tracks, I lost my place in my speech. Gone was my confidence. Gone was the slick tone to my words. I stood there—*speechless!* From where I stood, I saw Terry. His mouth was ajar, and he appeared to be frozen in disbelief.

Suddenly the most intense blue light surrounded me! It was like a strobe light, flashing all around me. "What is this?" I thought. Like lightning, it was dramatic and hard to overlook. "Why is no one, not even Terry, reacting to it?"

I managed to compose myself and get through my speech. I concluded it on a lukewarm note. The crowd went wild with applause. Obviously, they were relieved that I was done. That didn't bother me as much as the lingering question in my mind: "What happened to me on the platform? Whose voice had I heard?"

Then the oddest thing happened. An elderly man made his way to the base of the platform and met me as I made my exit. "That was some light show you put on!" he crowed. I stopped in my tracks and shook. I knew in that moment whose voice I had heard—*Jesus'*!

Born again

As we drove back home to Hollywood that day, I told Terry about my platform experience with Jesus. I shared how I knew that I wasn't supposed to be doing these New Age power talks anymore.

As Terry and I were sitting on the couch in our apartment that evening, we audibly heard the word *Jesus*. With it came a rush of power—like a wind—hitting us, knocking us to the floor!

We must have lost consciousness for several minutes. When we awoke, we got up on our knees, crying and asking the Lord to be with us. I felt that same loving presence that I used to feel at Grandpa's.

In an instant, joy flooded our lives. We stayed up three consecutive nights and talked like kids having a slumber party. The joy of the Lord replaced every bit of worry about walking away from L.A., TV, and the motivational speaking circuit. It had to be the joy of the Lord, for I had just turned my back on making a lucrative fifteen hundred dollars per talk, with all expenses paid! In the days to follow, our cupboards were bare and our bank account was dwindling, yet we were at peace as never before. *We had Jesus!*

Jesus and everything else

Yes, we had Jesus, but where did we go from there? To Canada! That is where the CBC television network picked up for a new season the shows I had taped for *Beyond Reason*. This was an opportunity to survive.

In my state of euphoria over new financial opportunity and the chance at TV notoriety, I did not pause to consider that I was headed right back into psychic activity.

I just did not associate this game show with "psychic" even though I was hired as the psychic to compete with an astrologer and a handwriting expert to get clues to figure out who the mystery guest would be. There was no one around us to point out that we must walk away from the old, especially psychic activity.

The scary part is that we now considered ourselves "Christians," but I was also doing psychic consultations from a hotel room. It was scary how people saw us! One well-known, award-winning pastry chef baked a cake on which was a frosted version of me doing a reading and Terry standing nearby with green "frosted bucks" in his hand!

I made appearances in Toronto based on the hit series. I did numerous seminars and workshops on the positive powers of the mind. I even published a book called *Your Supernatural Mind* and went on an international tour with it throughout Canada and Great Britain.

Despite the fact that things seemed to be going great, nothing seemed to work out. Now that we considered ourselves Christians we prayed, but no matter how much we wanted to go forward, things seemed to be spiraling downward. We did not know that we were still walking in disobedience to God's Word and that He was not honoring our activities or lifestyle.

On the book tour to England, the books got water-logged on the ship and were ruined. So I arrived on shore with no books to promote. The series in Canada went off the air. Soon thereafter, my books no longer were "current" and were replaced by others. Our passport time expired, and it was time to leave Canada. We left the country to seek work in the United States. This time we did not look for opportunities for me to be a psychic celebrity, but anything else that would aid in our survival.

The Witness From Hell

During the height of my public career as a practicing psychic, I was very well known for being on the daily TV series, *Beyond Reason*. One afternoon as Terry and I were standing in the lounge car of the train, a stranger came up to us. He was a middle-aged, rotund man.

The conversation started off innocently enough, with the stranger recognizing me from my TV series and talking with Terry and me about trains and the lovely day. Thinking that that this friendly stranger was interested in the two of us as human beings, we opened up and naturally let down our guard.

Suddenly, without warning, this friendly stranger turned ice cold and moved in for the kill, with, "Well, Sandra, you seem mighty happy with yourself about your psychic TV series, but after you die, you won't be so happy—in hell!"

The stranger's words cut through us like a knife. I felt betrayed! This man had bated me with kind words, then pierced my soul with words of hate. He had mentioned Jesus, but after his words of condemnation and hate, I wanted to hear no part of his Jesus! I walked away. The sad thing was—instead of leading us *to* Jesus, this angry and hateful man drove us *from* Jesus!

REFLECTIONS

I NOW SEE THAT during the season of our searching, Terry and I needed not witnesses from hell, condemning us, but witnesses from heaven—encouraging us in the ways of our newfound faith. Recently at a church seminar someone asked me, "How come you did not know that you were still practicing something sinful—in being a professional psychic—after you became born again?" My response has been, "If you are lost, you are lost!" You might accept Jesus as Lord and even become a new creation in Christ, but if there is no one telling you how to walk the walk, you are likely to fall back or pursue old ways. Terry and I found Jesus, but we still needed to find discipling in order to walk in His ways—and away from the New Age and occult! Terry and I were undiscipled and unchurched.

WHAT CAN BE DONE?

PERHAPS YOU KNOW a loved one or friend or even a stranger you have met who has come to Christ but is persisting in their old ways. Do not be confused and think that they are *not* a new creature in Christ. They just need to be shown how to walk the new walk in Christ, which will involve giving up former habits, ways, and certain behaviors. This will involve learning what God's Word says about their old sinful habits. They may need to have a pastor teach them. It may involve getting acquainted with how God views things (such as what He considers sin). That may entail them attending a new believers class or going to pastoral counseling.

As a minister, I have counseled many who have been in the occult and New Age. A sizable number of them have been former witches and psychics. They have needed to learn what is acceptable to God and what isn't, especially if they have been used to activities of the mind that have gone against God, such as mind reading, fortune-telling, consulting discarnate spirits, and doing incantations. All new converts who have been in the occult/New Age or who have been influenced by it in any way need to know that they will need to walk away from their old ways and adapt new ways of living that please Christ and are in Christ. A good place to begin is for them to attend:

- church

- counseling

- a new believers class in the church

- mentoring sessions

- interest or cell groups through church

Terry and I had no church, no pastoral care, and no immediate friends who were plugged in to a church. We were adrift and cut off. We did not even mention to our families who were scattered across the country of our born-again experience, so how could they know to guide us?

If you have someone in your family who has accepted Christ but is still pursuing old ways, the worst thing you can do is scold him or her. That would send him further back into the arms of Satan, further distancing him not only from you, but also from the Lord! Instead, offer love and encouragement that you and Jesus love them. Encourage them to get into God's Word. Buy them a good, easy-to-read Bible with sizable print. Take them or encourage them to get to church. Acting in the force of God will help pull them to God!

Avoid "gourmet sin" reasoning

When I was lost, I truly thought that what I did was for the good of mankind. I did not see my professional practices—such as TV appearances and psychic consultations—as sin. Years after I came to the Lord, I reminded Him in prayer that I hadn't used tarot cards or crystal balls. In other words, I was saying to God, "My style of 'psychic' was a cut above the others." To which He replied in that still, small voice, "Daughter, there is no such thing as gourmet sin."

You might have a loved one or someone you know who is following an occult/New Age mind-set and lifestyle. They might even be choosing that way of life, believing that it is OK because they are good people with good intentions. But God's Word tells us, "All our righteousnesses are like filthy rags" (Isa. 64:6). We live in a fallen world due to Adam's Fall.

Keep on praying for your loved one. When you talk with that lost or confused loved one, always keep pointing to the loving God who loves them. Point to Jesus the Son who died for them so they can live for eternity. Never stop reminding them that only Jesus is "the way, the truth, and the life" (John 14:6). It is only through Jesus that they will get to heaven.

The sore spot of church

During this season, the issue of church was a sore spot for us. We wanted to go, but what church would have us? Every time we turned on the radio, we heard the voices of preachers condemning psychics and occult practitioners. The last thing we wanted was to walk into a church full of hate and finger-pointing and feel unwelcome. So we avoided church, but avoiding church hurt us and bothered us to the core!

After a year of living in Toronto, Canada, with doors closing on us, the season of "Sandra, the celebrity psychic" was over. Little did we know that a new season was beginning—one of hard labor in a Boston bakery.

PRAYER STRATEGIES

HOW DO YOU PRAY for someone who has accepted Jesus but is still living in old sinful ways? Pray that he gets the discipline he needs through the church to know the difference between darkness (or the counterfeit) and the right way to live in Christ. Pray that he gets to a church that will disciple him. Pray that the Lord will make you an instrument to mentor and lovingly guide him in the ways of Christ.

TALKING IT OVER

1. Discuss and get group reaction to this question: why is it so important for new believers to be discipled in Christ?

2. Encourage everyone in your discussion group to share their testimony and how God's hand was on them, even when they were at their most sinful or "lost" state.

CHAPTER 6

~

ROLLING IN
THE DOUGH?

He will yet fill your mouth with laughing, and
your lips with rejoicing.

—Job 8:21

MY JOURNEY

THE SIGN READ: HELP WANTED: ONE BAKER
AND ONE COUNTER CASHIER. HUSBAND
AND WIFE PREFERRED. It caught our eyes since
my husband Terry and I were out of work. We decided
to move to Boston, an environment similar to Toronto.
The problem was that we arrived with little money and

no jobs. The jobs we interviewed for by phone never came to fruition.

We went into the bakery, applied, and were hired on the spot—Terry as the baker (with little prior experience) and I as the counter help (with even less prior experience). Obviously they were as desperate for help as we were for income!

From the fruit cellar to a new day

Our dreams of rolling *in* the dough from New Age notoriety turned to rolling the dough! With nothing in sight but hard work in a bakery—with a schedule and chores that were new turf to us—our dreams were fading fast. Our day began with us rising early in our rented apartment, which was really a one-room basement rental (more like a fruit cellar), separated by a thin plywood wall from another just like it.

Don't cry for me, Argentina!

I wouldn't have minded living in the basement during our bakery days, except for one thing—the sound of a cracked female voice singing, "Don't Cry For Me, Argentina!" It came from the other side of the thin plywood wall separating our "apartment" from the neighbors'—a man and his wife, who had a habit of singing off key when she cooked. Unfortunately she cooked often.

Flat out in God's Word

As we endured choice selections from *Evita* in the evenings, we had to lie flat on our backs on our one and only piece of furniture—a futon. There we took turns reading from our one and only book—the Bible. "OK," I would announce to Terry, "Find me something about God prospering us!" Terry would thumb quickly through the book with no time to lose lest we lose faith within two minutes. "How about Philippians 4:19?" Terry asked, and together we looked it up and read aloud:

> And my God shall supply all your need according
> to His riches in glory by Christ Jesus.
> —Philippians 4:19

God began to supply all our need in ways unexpected!

God in unusual circumstances

Our daily walk to work was down dark and shadowy streets. I knew God was bringing me new reasons to smile at the bakery, but our living arrangement and the walk to work each morning made me question Him all over again, asking, "Are you there, Lord?"

Every morning we did the same thing. Because it was a season of unknowns (new city, new vocation, new style of living), the "sameness" of each day offered stability. Terry baked croissants, using a Julia Child cookbook we checked out from the library. I worked the counter. As Terry got the dough ready, I would stack the counter with coffee cups, sugar, and creamer packets. I loaded the glass counter cases with almond and chocolate and spinach croissants, bran muffins, and a variety of sugar and iced cookies.

At 6:00 a.m. a cavalcade of "regulars" came in, one after another. First came Lou the neighborhood barber, whose gruff request for coffee sounded more like the threat from a gangster. Then came sparrow-like Priscilla, the grandma who would whisper her desire for two muffins toasted, making sure she added, "I pray you'll have a wonderful day, dear." The afternoon brought moms with active preschoolers, causing me to laugh at the unpredictable kids as I served up hot apple croissants, milk, and hot tea. Our days were not only full of bakery goodies, but the people who devoured them. I soon discovered that we were not only working in a bakery business, but also a people business.

Happy foursome

The afternoon also brought four adults who called themselves the "Happy Foursome." They were mentally challenged and lived in a nearby assisted living facility right in the heart of Brookline Village.

One afternoon, a tall woman from the group began banging her fist on the counter. "I need the fattest sweet roll you have. I'm on a diet, and dieting makes me hungry!" The young woman next to her was blowing smoke rings in my face. "She's a talented smoker," grinned a young man whose knit hat was pulled so tightly upon his head that his ears stood out. The other member of the group was studying the sky through the window.

Over the course of several months the label "Happy Foursome" faded as I learned their names and began to see personality traits of my daily friends. The tall outspoken lady, who ate because she was on a diet, was Claude. She laughed a lot and talked with her hands. Sharon, the smoke ring artist, made sure she blew her rings outside. Sharon was usually quiet and smiled a lot. Billy was the animated young man with the hat and ears. He was eager to please. Bob was the art enthusiast, always pointing to the colors of the sky and the leaves and birds.

As the days progressed, I began to see beyond their faces and actions into their hearts—hearts that began to touch my own with a kindness that gave me great hope during a difficult time.

Chased by a shadowy figure

One dark morning as we walked to work, I spied a shadowy figure that was different from the normal ones of trees, hedges, bushes, and gloomy buildings. This one had arms and legs and wore a black cloak. It rose up from a pile of sticks to the side of the street and groaned. I found my throat constricting, and the only thing that I would whisper to Terry was, "Be cool. A man is following us."

"Right," whispered Terry in cooperation.

With no time to lose, I shot ahead of Terry and ran like a jackrabbit. Terry was now on my heels, yelling, "I thought you said to be cool!"

I made a sharp right turn into the police station with Terry not far behind—and behind him, the shadowy, cloaked figure catching up with us. Once Terry and I were inside the police station, I reported the strange figure that appeared to be galloping after us.

"Oh, him," said a couple of officers in unison. "That's Beau." It seems that Beau, who had a house but liked to sleep in the streets, was making sure we had a bodyguard escort that morning. We were told he liked to follow people in the dark, early morning hours, making sure that everyone was safe. We left, not exactly comforted, but with one more reason to smile. When the bakery door swung open that morning, Beau was at the door with his hand on the bell, clanging it and singing, "Dashing through the snow!"

God did not make a mistake

Soon I began to see that God was showing me something. He not only was supplying all our need, but He had not made a mistake at all! He was surprising me with reasons to laugh and smile again in the least likely of places—a bakery, where the work was unglamorous and the hours were back-breakingly long!

Shake off the dust

You know it is time to make a change when people look at you on the street, begin to salivate, and say, "I'm reminded of a sweet roll!" After a year of the season of the bakery, Terry and I knew that we had to shake off the dust—or, in our case, pastry flour—and move on. This had been a season of working to merely survive and not to establish ourselves as bakery experts.

We knew we couldn't go back to Canada, for there was no TV series to go back to. So we did the next best thing—we moved *near* Canada, to the city of Rochester, New York. To us this seemed a logical move. I could go to Canada and do psychic consultations and Terry could find work and make a living. What we didn't know was that God had other plans in store for us, including a Christian witness who helped get us to the right church.

REFLECTIONS

As I look back, I now see where the bakery appeared to be the bleakest experience ever. To go from a TV celebrity psychic to a klutzy (because I didn't know what I was doing) counter help in a bakery was very hard. Yet, in the experience I began to feel the very presence of God as never before. I now see that He was changing my attitude from "woe is me" to "how can I brighten your day?" As a result, I was blessed by so many people.

Questions I have received

I have been asked over and over again two basic "why would" questions by others. Below are the questions. I admit they have challenged my faith but have never rocked it.

1.   Why would God even bother reaching someone lost in the occult/New Age who has rejected His love?

My answer to this question draws from the powerful scripture that demonstrates God's unconditional love for us before we have made up our minds to accept Him:

> But God demonstrates His own love toward us,
> in that while we were still sinners, Christ died
> for us.
>
> —ROMANS 5:8

2. How could someone lost in the occult/New Age begin to feel God's love?

The key words are not *someone lost* but *God's love.* His love is stronger than the lost state in which one lives.

During the season of the bakery, I began to experience the Lord's increasing loving presence during my days at the front counter. As I dealt with customers at the cash register, quite often I would feel a surge of joy and would know that Jesus was right there with me. He was reaching down to me in my "lostness" and was touching me with His love. Some say that God requires that we come to Him and repent first, and then He will touch us with His love. Nowhere in God's Word is this stated. Otherwise, why would God so love the world that He sent to us His only begotten Son? (See John 3:16.) God is love. (See 1 John 4:8.)

WHAT CAN BE DONE?

HOW DO YOU PRAY for loved ones who are lost and struggling at the same time? There is a chance that they might be so angry with God that they reject Him. There is the risk that they are blaming Him for their struggles and pains, so why should they accept, or even want to hear, your "points for Christ"?

What can be done to minister to your lost loved ones without turning them away from God? Make room for the Holy Spirit to go to work on them. Give them room and time. God does. Why should your agenda for them to be saved be any more pressing than His? When I first went to work in the bakery, I was mad at God. How could He do this to me? Where is He?

God positions us for the best to come!

Little did I know that this bottoming-out period of being where I didn't want to be was actually God's positioning me for the best that He had for Terry and me. In the next chapter I will share how I encountered a Christian witness who led the way for the best yet to come.

PRAYER STRATEGIES

THE LAST THING LOST people will want to hear, especially in their struggles, is news of an angry God who could send them to hell. Certainly hell is real, and those who reject Jesus will go there. But Jesus came to offer us life and life abundantly. (See John 10:10.) Why not, like Jesus at the well (see next chapter), offer new hope and new life in Him? Your lost loved one will certainly respond to the power of the good news of new hope and new life in Him over any power of the bad news of hell.

TALKING IT OVER

DISCUSS CREATIVE WAYS TO encourage people in Christ in a variety of situations. Role-playing is encouraged, where one person will be the Christian witness and the other will be a person lost in the New Age/occult. Have the Christian witness speak to him or her about Jesus and how there is a better way (Jesus) and a better life for them in Him.

Discuss why at times things have to get worse before they can get better in the life of someone lost in the New Age/occult before they come to Christ.

CHAPTER 7

~

WITNESS ON A BRIDGE

So He came to a city of Samaria which is called
Sychar, near the plot of ground that Jacob gave to
his son Joseph. Now Jacob's well was there. Jesus
therefore, being wearied from His journey, sat
thus by the well. It was about the sixth hour. A
woman of Samaria came to draw water. Jesus said
to her, "Give Me a drink."

—JOHN 4:5–7

God had moved inwardly in our lives in the season of
the bakery. Now He was moving in our lives in Rochester,
New York! From the moment we arrived, we began plans
to move again to Los Angeles! We knew that we had to
get back to L.A. Why? In L.A. we had friends, and we
had contacts in the show business arena where I could use

my union cards to bring in some money (working in the movies). We both prayed and knew that God wanted us there, for whatever other reasons. Just making plans to move to L.A. brought us a sense of peace—and expectation. We knew that God was up to something.

By now I had all but given up doing psychic consultations and media as a psychic. I was doing temporary work and Terry managed a bookstore. We were reading the Bible, particularly the New Testament, more and more. We began to pay attention to the still, small voice of God, guiding us back to L.A.

The missing peace

As soon as we moved into an L.A. apartment, Terry began work in retail. From my psychic media days I had union cards for TV and movie work. They enabled me to earn a good living as a screen extra. I took up something stable—like acting!

What was still missing in our lives was church. Intimidated by the thought of church people not accepting us due to our occult past, we continued to stay at home on Sunday mornings. Church was definitely a missing piece to our lives—or I should say "missing peace"? We knew that our avoiding it was creating an aching hole within us.

On the other hand, nothing or no one could convince us to go to church! We didn't have the energy to begin to explain our past to others. We were born again, but we just did not fit into the cookie-cutter pattern of life that most Christians seemed to have! Meanwhile, God was setting up a divine appointment for me with a lady who would forever change things.

The encounter

I was on the set of a TV sitcom one afternoon, resting between rehearsals, when a lady who was also an extra came up to me and sat beside me. "Wow," she said, admiring my cross necklace, "That is so pretty! I'm a believer, too!" Before I could even respond to that, she popped the one question I dreaded to hear, "Where is your home church?"

Silence followed—uncomfortable silence. I did not know how to answer her. Terry and I were still living unchurched. We were unchurched and ashamed of it. I felt like I was the only Christian in the world living like this. I felt as if my world was behind a wall that was cut off from life and Christ Himself.

God is the maker of divine appointments for us!

I squirmed in my seat before this stranger who was probing my church life. I couldn't lie. To lie about my Christian walk was hardly a good thing! After having served the devil as a psychic, the last thing I wanted to do was to serve him again by lying about my Christian faith.

The stranger was waiting for an answer. Then, in her style of not waiting too long, she jumped in, "Hey, *no* church is perfect! You don't even have to *like* some of the people! But if you miss church and don't go, you miss so much and that would be sad."

The stranger's voice was kind, and her eyes twinkled as if excited about the news she was bringing to me. In that moment, I felt that she was with me in my state of isolation from the church. *She understood how I felt!*

Her next question would have normally offended me. Because it followed her kind and caring approach to me, I did not mind it. She persisted kindly: "Do you go to church at all?" My answer, "Not yet," did not seem to affect her. She only became *kinder*! And, oddly, I became more *comfortable*!

Here was someone meeting me and sitting by me in the middle of where I was—unchurched and ashamed of it. Without blinking, she said, "Well, Jesus loves you. Do you know that?" Then she added with a promise so firm that I had to take notice, "I want you to know that I will be praying that you find the right church. It's out there, you know."

The kind stranger's parting words to me were said so unconditionally lovingly that they placed me in a position of new hope! I went from former psychic to child of the King! "Remember," she reminded me as we parted, "you belong to Jesus now, and that means that you belong in His church!" Not only did I feel new hope, but I also felt new peace. This encounter with the stranger reminded me that Terry and I were worth something in the Lord's eyes!

God would see to it that we would get into the right church. "This lady on the bridge would be praying for the right church for us," I thought. Just knowing that made all the difference.

REFLECTIONS

SINCE THOSE DAYS, I have learned that at least one third of the general population is unchurched.[1] I have also learned from doing pastoral counseling (talking with former unchurched men and women) that it is common for the unchurched to experience feelings of isolation.[2]

I met the woman who convinced me to seek out a church on what I have come to call a spiritual bridge. I call it a spiritual bridge because it was a mutual place where I could cross into her world of the church. This provided a feeling of safety, which enabled me to listen to what she had to say. I had not felt pressured—just visited. What harm would it do to listen to her? What did I have to lose in seeking a church?

The woman's actions of love and encouragement were *bridge builders*. They built a bridge that pointed me to the Lord. Here are some *bridge builders* that can connect you with that lost loved one or even a stranger as you point them to Jesus:

WHAT CAN BE DONE?

WHERE DO YOU BEGIN to reach someone who is lost in the occult/New Age? Begin with the model of Jesus who loved sinners as they were. Although they were wrong and most of them were probably disgusting, Jesus loved them as they were, then touched them and healed them. In Scripture, we see Jesus viewing a group of people first, then being moved with compassion to do something about their situations. Then He healed them: "And when Jesus went out He saw a great multitude; and He was moved with compassion for them, and healed their sick" (Matt. 14:14).

> **BUILDING A BRIDGE:**
>
> *Like Jesus, come alongside those who are lost.*

1. Be approachable

Jesus never *ran from* anyone. He was there *for* them. He was there *with* them as He was with the woman at the well.

Consider that Jesus even crossed into Samaria, a land known for its tainted inhabitants who were considered sinful and to be avoided.[3] When He saw the woman at the well who approached Him, He, being holy, did not run from her. That would have been a *bridge wash-out*—or something that would have disconnected Him from her.

BUILDING A BRIDGE:

Like Jesus, meet the lost where they are.

The stranger on the set of the TV studio, like Jesus with the woman at the well, did not run or get up and move away from me once she found out that I was unchurched. Nor did she scorn me in any way. She remained near me, like Jesus had with the woman at the well, and she began to dialogue with me. She met me on a bridge of connection, came alongside me where I was, and then pointed the way to hope in Jesus through His love.

2. Dialogue with love

Notice in the passage in John 4:5–7 that Jesus does not lecture the sinful woman at the well.

Nor did Jesus condemn the woman at the well. Had He done so, she most likely would have fled. Had the lady at the TV studio lectured me or condemned me to hell for being unchurched, I too would have fled and avoided church all the more.

3. Encourage a future in Christ

What did the lady on the set of the TV studio do that was so special? She listened.

> **BUILDING A BRIDGE:**
> *Like Jesus, listen to people.*

Scripture reveals that Jesus listened to people. When the synagogue official came up to Him, no matter how busy He was, He stopped and listened. (See Matthew 9:18.) When the two blind men cried out for Him, Jesus paused to listen. (See Matthew 9:27–28.) Jesus encouraged, instead of discouraged, the lost and those in the midst of crisis.

Like Jesus, the lady on the set of the TV studio took time with me, listened to my cry, and offered help and hope. That made all the difference in the world to me. I was able to move with confidence, backed by the love of Jesus shared with me on the bridge of connection, as I considered stepping out from being *unchurched* to *churched*.

Bridges of hope

There are things you can always do to encourage a future in Christ as you come alongside that person on a spiritual bridge. You can invite him or her to:

- come to your church or church in general;

- read something you share (gently and lovingly);

- express their feelings;

- listen to you as you share something marvelous and loving about how good God is (without preaching).

Make room for the Holy Spirit

As you meet that lost loved one on a bridge that could connect him or her to Christ, you are not alone! The Holy Spirit is *with* you and *in* you, empowering you to point that lost loved one to Christ. The Holy Spirit is at work on the bridge, helping the lost person to be aware of Christ.

The woman who met me on the bridge that afternoon made room for the Holy Spirit to do His work to lead me to repentance. Notice in the story of the woman at the well in John 4:7–29 that nowhere does it mention that Jesus forced the woman to repent or to even move out of her present situation. Jesus simply shared with the woman of *living water*. He told her of eternal life in Him.

When you and I meet someone in a sinful situation or state of being lost, should we do no different than Jesus? As His ministers, we are in His ministry, and that is the ministry of spreading His love. The best way that can happen is on the bridge of connection, where you meet the person where they are and point to Christ.

4. Show His loving presence

Be willing to plant a seed in the life of the lost. Often that person whom we meet on the bridge will learn something about Jesus' love through our mere presence and the seeds of love and caring that we display. The lost may or may not receive Jesus on the spot, but they are watching us. What we do will influence them at some level. We can plant a powerful seed in their lives that will blossom in the right timing.

If people are ready to receive Jesus as their Lord and Savior on the spot, then that is wonderful. If they are not ready, it is still a wonderful thing! Why? You have met them where they are, just as Jesus did with the woman at the well and then pointed to the One who loved her best! You have planted seed that is alive and connected to Jesus the Vine. (See John 15:5.) You have become His ambassador. In God's Word, the apostle Paul reminds us:

> Now then, we are ambassadors for Christ, as though God were pleading through us.
>
> —2 CORINTHIANS 5:20

How can you lose when you share Jesus' love for that lost loved one, or friend, or even a stranger? And how can they lose when they are exposed to His unconditional love?

Bridge builders along the way

Consider when you finally accepted Jesus as your Savior. Prior to that moment, there might have been people along the way who guided you, influenced you, and even pointed you to that one crowning moment when you received Jesus. Those people, in pointing the way toward Jesus, met you on a bridge and were able to point you to Jesus Christ. They, like the woman on the set that day with me, positioned you for the salvation moment when you decided to accept Jesus Christ as Savior.

If you would like your very words and actions and attitude to be bridge builders that can connect with someone, then be aware that you can start today! You can be used greatly of God today to meet someone on a bridge and to point the way to Jesus!

Bridging the gap with Jesus

Scripture shows us something significant about moving in the love of Jesus. Consider when Jesus saw a group from afar and was moved with compassion: "And when Jesus went out He saw a great multitude; and He was moved with compassion for them, and healed their sick" (Matt. 14:14).

> **BUILDING A BRIDGE:**
>
> *Like Jesus, share His love and plant a seed that will blossom in due season.*

This passage of Scripture shows how Jesus moved in the expression of His love. Note that it says, "He was moved *with* compassion" (emphasis added). The words *moved with* are a key phrase. It is a descriptive participle that tells us that Jesus already had this kind of love operating from *within Him*. The word *with*, a preposition, relates to Jesus as an intrinsic part of Him as He moved.

Why is it important to know how Jesus moved with love? As believers in Christ, you and I move *in* Him or in His power. Scripture verifies this. Paul stated, "For in Him we live and move and have our being" (Acts 17:28).

It is essential to know that you and I, as *carriers* of the Spirit of Christ (who is love), are positioned to carry Christ's love and compassion. That means that we, as His carriers of love, can bridge the gap and reach the lost with His message of His love.

You and I, as believers, are *already* His vessels, equipped and ready to move in the same compassion as modeled by Jesus. Our love of Christ that we move in when we approach someone on the bridge will not be a "thing" that hits at us after we pray. Just as Jesus moved in love, so will we as we move in Jesus, pointing to Him!

Ask the Lord to empower you to reach someone today on the *bridge of connection*, using His love. Perhaps the best thing we can do for those around us influenced by the occult/New Age, to whatever degree, would be to do what Jesus did—to approach them where they are with love. The story to follow, a true one, is a testimony that God can work the impossible when we reach others with the love of Jesus.

PRAYER STRATEGIES

TAKE THESE PRAYER STRATEGIES of love.

- Pray that the Lord would make you an active vessel of His love as you approach people in their world today.

- Pray that the Lord would touch each person you encounter with His love.

- Pray for your lost loved ones and that this is the day (or week or month) when they will come closer to Jesus and enjoy a relationship with Him.

TALKING IT OVER

1. How would you meet these people on a bridge (relating to them where they are) and then point them to Jesus Christ? You do not have to force them to salvation, but perhaps just relate to them and then point them to Jesus and how He loves them:

   - an astrologer

   - someone who has no real belief in Christ

   - a practicing psychic

2. Your dear cousin, Theo, has dropped out of church due to hypocrisy and gossip. You would

like for him to come back to church. What do
you say to him?

3. How do you become an ambassador for Christ
in everyday situations?

CHAPTER 8

~

WELCOME TO CHURCH 101

I was glad when they said to me, "Let us go into the house of the LORD."

—PSALM 122:1

MY JOURNEY

ENTRY INTO CHURCH WAS a complete shock. It was nothing like the sleepy church of my youth. My last church service had been years ago. It wasn't over until stately Mrs. Higgans, with a hair bun as tall as a skyscraper, sang in a falsetto that could shatter glass.

We entered on a Sunday morning during the praise part of praise and worship. We were ushered near the front of a church with approximately two thousand members.

Before I could whisper to Terry, "This is too much! Let's get out of here!" we were already sandwiched in like two pieces of old cheese in a jiggling sandwich. A man on Terry's left was waving his arm wildly from left to right, and a woman on my right wore a hat that strangely resembled a flying saucer. With each bounce she took, the saucer tilted more toward my ear, as if getting ready to make a landing. "What in the world have we gotten ourselves into?" I thought.

What didn't happen

Did we go down front when the altar call was given? Heavens no! Although I had to admit there was something about this church that drew me. People seemed so happy and at peace. "What is it?" I wondered.

Three hours later, as Terry and I made our way across the parking lot, the early afternoon sun warmed my face, and it felt so good to be alive.

"The joy in that place was contagious!" I remarked to Terry. He nodded and smiled in agreement. As I climbed into our car, I remembered the friendly face of the official greeter, a woman in a smart lilac suit, who handed us a bulletin and said, "Hello. So glad to see you! Welcome!"

"So how do we let them know who we are and what we've been into?" I asked Terry. His smile disappeared with no response. How could we, with our pasts, ever fit in here?

What did happen

That night I was awakened by a loud noise. Startled, I sat up in bed. I shuddered, recalling the days of my psychic activity when I heard taps at night on the walls of my bedroom.

I sat silent in the dark of the room. I could hear Terry's breathing, but that wasn't it. There it was again! It was all around me, yet *in* me! I gripped the sides of my head. It felt like something—a machine—was boring a hole into my head! *The more it continued, the lighter and freer I felt!*

Exhausted, I fell back onto the bed and began to drift off. In a few minutes, I was aware that there was a figure standing at the foot of our bed—all lit up in white! Too sleepy to fully open my eyes, I gazed at the light and the first thought I had was, "Jesus?" And that was the last thought I had before I fully sank into a deep sleep.

Dawn of a new day

When I awoke the next morning, I had the memory of what I thought was a dream. Jesus had come into our bedroom and had caught snakes coming from my head. "Be gone in My name!" He commanded.

I will never know if the figure I saw at the end of our bed was just a part of my dream or Jesus actually making a visit. In either case, after the previous night, I knew that Jesus had done a deliverance of some kind on my psychic abilities, and I would never be able to practice them again.

"How are you feeling?" asked Terry, bringing me coffee in bed.

Without soft-soaping anything, I merely replied, "We belong in church." Then I proceeded to share my middle-of-the-night deliverance.

Deliverance in church

The very next weekend, there was another altar call. This time, Terry and I went down to the front and had prayers of deliverance prayed over us. We publicly confessed and accepted Jesus Christ as our Lord and Savior. Two weeks later we received the baptism of the Holy Spirit. Not only did I no longer have any desire to do psychic activity, but I also found myself changed! I no longer *could* do it!

Equally remarkable was the fact that after I received the baptism of the Holy Spirit, I was able to sense things in a new way and to a greater extent! I could see more clearly than ever, only now, as God directed me. "You,

Sandra" stated the senior pastor during a church service one day, "are a prophet of the Lord, and you will never go back to your former psychic self!"

Close encounters

That experience did not mean that the road would be easy. In fact, there were some in the church who knew of my occult background and decided, despite my repentance, deliverance, and new blessing of being a prophet of the Lord, that I needed policing. "After all," whispered some, "With her past, we must be careful."

Then there was the supervisor of the prayer line where I worked, who thought it best for all if I resign and hand in my prayer badge. "People are uncomfortable with your past," she said.

"But why?" I asked.

I had been reading the writings of the apostle Paul, particularly from Romans 8:1: "There is therefore now no condemnation to those who are in Christ Jesus, who do not walk according to the flesh, but according to the Spirit." This gave me the confidence to answer her: "That is *not* the God I serve! My God offers redemption and salvation and forgiveness for sinners!"

That did not satisfy my supervisor. She arranged for me to meet with the associate pastor in charge of prayer activities "to explain myself." Terry and I went together.

To our surprise, the associate pastor took our side. He cited God's Word:

> For all have sinned and fall short of the glory of God.
>
> —ROMANS 3:23

I left that session free! I felt so loved by a God who desired that I live a new life in Jesus Christ!

REFLECTIONS

ALTHOUGH OUR BACKGROUND IN New Age may have been intense, we were probably not that different in many ways from a sizeable number of people who are entering or reentering the church today. Without a strong biblical background, the newcomer often brings with him or her subtle influences of New Age and the occult.

When Terry and I entered the local church, we found ourselves on foreign turf in a land with its own language and mode of behavior. We needed help! I learned such phrases as "a check in my spirit," which means hesitancy; "touch and agree," which means to pray in agreement; and "to lift up," meaning to keep someone in prayer.

I began to fear speaking up with my opinions, lest someone find my thoughts tainted because of my dark occult background. When groups asked for a volunteer to open in prayer, I held back. My confidence was not there! "Who am I—a former psychic—to pray for anyone?" I thought.

All too soon I began to see that I was carrying the baggage of fear and my own bias toward church people. Many of them were very kind, but some held back for fear that some of my dark past would rub off on them.

By the "removing" of your mind

The fact that I had been a New Age motivational speaker at large conventions seemed to be nonthreatening to people. But whenever some remembered me as a former psychic who did readings and visited haunted houses, they backed away from me, afraid and on their guard.

This hurt, because I was not a thing, but a person capable of love and who needed love from my new church family. It also hurt because I was trying to walk a new walk, and some kept picturing me back on my old sinful path.

I was also concerned. I was convinced that God created our minds to think, to reason, and to perceive, not to vegetate. As long as I was not directing my mind to do psychic activity, what was to be feared by the fact that I had a sharp mind? The associate pastor referred Terry and me to the scripture that tells us to renew our minds, not *remove* them (as some would have advised me):

I beseech you therefore, brethren, by the mercies of God, that you present your bodies a living sacrifice, holy, acceptable to God, which is your reasonable service. And do not be conformed to this world, but be transformed by the renewing of your mind, that you may prove what is that good and acceptable and perfect will of God.

—ROMANS 12:1–2

The amazing thing to Terry and me was that many of these church people had pasts that were perhaps just as shocking, or more, than ours. Many had been into drugs or alcohol and even crime. Some informed us that drugs and alcohol were substances that could be thrown away, but who could prove that we had gotten rid of dark forces? Had they not read the section of the Bible that speaks of us being a "new creature in Christ"?

Therefore, if anyone is in Christ, he is a new creation; old things have passed away; behold, all things have become new.

—2 CORINTHIANS 5:17

Who's who?

Over the years I have discovered basic myths and the truths that counter them related to psychics and occultists and even prophets. If these myths are cleared up, perhaps people will know "who is who" and understand, by God's Word, that psychics, once they come to Christ, are no longer psychics or contagious dark forces.

MYTH: Once a psychic or occultist/New Ager, always one.

TRUTH: When you and I come to Christ, we become a new creation:

> Therefore, if anyone *is* in Christ, he *is* a new creation; old things have passed away; behold, all things have become new.
> —2 CORINTHIANS 5:17, EMPHASIS ADDED

The late Andrew Murray, respected pastor and theologian, has stated in his book, *Abide in Christ*, that as "new creations in Christ" we are the very branches of Him, and now are *in* Him.[1] So how, if we are in Him, can we sin? How might a believer in Christ (or one redeemed and delivered from the occult/New Age) still be a psychic? How can the new creation in Christ be also the old, marred creature in Adam? To be both would basically deny the power of the cross and its redeeming power over sin. Murray has cited God's Word to reinforce this truth:

In him is no sin. Whosoever abideth in him sin-
neth not.

—1 JOHN 3:5–6, KJV

What about backsliding? Could a new creation
in Christ ever be tempted to go back to the occult and
psychic activities? I have asked myself that and have been
asked that after my talks. Murray has reminded us further
that though we as humans have the choice, if we keep
abiding in Christ, we walk in "His all-sufficient power"
over our weakness.[2]

MYTH: Being psychic and prophetic are the same
thing.

TRUTH: According to the *New International
Dictionary of New Testament Theology*, there is a difference
between a "soothsayer" (now often known as a "psychic")
and a "prophet." The word *prophet*, according to *The New
Unger's Bible Dictionary*, is "One who is divinely inspired
to communicate God's will to His people and to disclose
the future to them."[3] The word *prophet* has Greek roots
from the word here in transliterated form as *prophetes*.
Its stem *phe* means "to say, proclaim, which has religious
connotation, and the prefix *pro* is a temporal adverb that
has the meaning of before, or in advance."[4] A *prophet* is
"one who predicts or tells beforehand."[5] In other words, a

prophet foretells the things of God, from God. God is at the center of a prophet's activities.

So now one might ask, Are not psychics gifted with the same gift and power? Our source for the clarification to this question is God's Word, which condemns psychics or soothsayers:

> There shall not be found among you anyone who makes his son or his daughter pass through the fire, or one who practices witchcraft, or a soothsayer, or one who interprets omens, or a sorcerer, or one who conjures spells, or a medium, or a spiritist, or one who calls up the dead. For all who do these things are an abomination to the LORD, and because of these abominations the LORD your God drives them out from before you.
> —DEUTERONOMY 18:10–12

This above scripture reveals to us that soothsayer or "psychic power" is not God's power. Its source is the self. Because it is not of God, it operates under the lower demonic realms and certainly not the holy realm of God.

In the days of my psychic career, many other psychics predicted my future. Most kept speaking of scenes where they saw me "one day in front of a variety of audiences with a book in my hand." Not one of them could say what I was doing in front of those audiences, nor what the mysterious book was! Not one mentioned God! I caution you to be aware, there are many psychics who now use the word *God* but are not in Jesus Christ. They are false and can be called charlatans or even false prophets.

It stands to reason that if psychic activity is *not* of God, or even blessed by God, then why would psychic practitioners expect to recognize God's plans or the special things that He has hidden? Why would God honor someone practicing what He has come against as evil? There are mysteries of God that He holds for the future, safe from the eyes of the occultists, soothsayers, and psychics.

Psychic activity bypasses the need for God]

To put it in my own basic terms from experience, psychic activity is a forced view of something that is directed (self-willed) by the mind in an altered state. It is feeling or sensing something beyond a mere hunch or intuitive gut feeling. It is directed by the mind in an altered state to feel or sense something about an object, person, or event. Notice how I referred to psychic activity as the use of a *sense*. This is not to say it is a mere hunch or moment of intuition. All of us, being humans with emotions and a sense of people and our surroundings, will get a mere sense of things or a feeling. That is not psychic.

Psychic activity will involve actually going into that person's location or emotions—much like a surgeon's tool—and get data beyond what meets the eye. It will involve forcing oneself into someone's life and sensing what he or she is really feeling, thinking, doing, or what they are about to encounter. Not only is this a human-to-human intrusion, but also it is playing God.

Can you see why God does not honor this kind of activity? If psychics do such acts as usurping God, why would there be need for God Himself?

The *New International Dictionary of New Testament Theology* states: "The prophet must be clearly distinguished from the soothsayer."[6] This same source has mentioned that through the ages, prophets have, like soothsayers, spoken with reason.[7] This means both have been able to get details that make sense. But it goes on to stress that there is a line drawn between the two:

> Soothsaying [or psychic], as in the case of prophecy, is never a timeless truth of universal validity, but a message directed to definite, individual events.[8]

We might surmise from this that the prophetic word, unlike the psychic prediction, carries God's overview of the individual, his life, and God's plan for him. Another source, *Handbook of Today's Religions*, refers to the fact that the Bible has scriptures calling such powers as not of God.[9] This source states, "In conclusion, there are many different names for fortunetellers, or mediums [or psychics as well]. By whatever name, they are completely condemned by the Bible.[10] God calls them detestable in Deuteronomy 18:11–12. One who practices such things was condemned to death under Old Testament theocracy. (See Leviticus 20:6, 27.)"[11]

There are Greek origins of the word *soothsayer*. *Soothsayer* originates from *mantis*, derived from the transliterated Greek word *mainomai*, which means "to rage, to be out of one's senses, to be in ecstasy." It is self-willed and directed from altered levels of the mind (hence, the meaning ecstasy) and not from the will of God directing it.[12]

Praying mantis?

In the days when I was confused and trying to be both a psychic and unchurched Christian, you might say I was a "praying mantis." To be a little or part of both is like being a "little" pregnant! Bear in mind that the very God who curses the activity cannot bless it at the same time.

Both the psychic and the prophet of God are seers. But one—the soothsayer or psychic—sees with limitation (and often inaccurately) from the depraved and marred curse under Adam; while the other, the prophet, a new creature in Christ sees *not* through self will, but through God's directed will for God's purposes.

Can a psychic turn into a prophet?

No. But there has been more than one psychic to "turn a profit!" A psychic is someone operating under Adam's Fall and curse, so why would he or she just be able to at will turn into a prophet? They need to come to Christ first, repent, and be changed.

The Theological Wordbook mentions how repentance is change, with the origin of the words *to change* coming from the Greek term *metanoia*.[13] *The Theological Wordbook* has further elaborated on the fact that Jesus sought change in people's thinking:

> With the presence of Christ in the world people needed to understand who He was and why He had come and this demanded a change in their thinking. So the word metanoia accurately expresses how Israel was to respond to Christ and His message.[14]

God's Word serves as a model for repenting and receiving Jesus Christ as Savior. It shows how when one does so, there is change. The person will become a branch belonging to (and fed by) the Vine, Jesus Christ:

Abide in Me, and I in you. As the branch cannot
bear fruit of itself, unless it abides in the vine, neither can you, unless you abide in Me.

—JOHN 15:4

Once anyone has come to Christ, he or she, being now
in Him, can receive all that He is as His branch. Andrew
Murray focused on this phenomenon in his book, *Abide
in Christ*.[15] When I came back to Christ, I turned away
from my sin and became a new creation in Christ. Now,
in Christ Jesus and experiencing all that I am in Him,
why would I ever want to go back to the dark and the
despair and horror of a past without Him?

WHAT CAN BE DONE?

THE CHURCH IS PROCLAIMING the end-time harvest of
souls coming. Many churches are doing a wonderful job
of reaching the lost, showing the love of Jesus, and inviting those lost (of any kind) to come to Christ.

But can more be done in the church itself to integrate
the lost occultist/New Ager into the church, so that he or
she no longer feels left out and uneasy? Can more be done
with the former occultist/New Ager to make him or her
more at peace with their present and future, despite their
horrific past?

How to integrate the two

Perhaps the church should examine barriers that both camps (the already churched and the newcomers coming in from the occult/New Age) have built against the other—and then come up with ways in which to tear them down. Below are a couple of approaches that appear to work.

The power of fellowship

One powerful thing that broke the ice for Terry and me and the church was fellowship. We decided to join groups. When we did, we found ourselves included in a variety of activities—some were study groups, others were sports and fun activities like bowling or even going out to breakfast. Church members got to know us as people, and we got to know them as people, too!

The power of group discipleship

One particular church we attended invited me to give my testimony, followed by a question-and-answer session with the pastor's insights to follow. This was valuable, as it let me inform and educate from my own perspective about the occult and New Age. In letting me do this, the church intensified and broadened its members' wisdom.

For members who had loved ones in the occult/ New Age, hearing someone's testimony empowered them to be able to minister to their loved ones. The question and answer session allowed them to dispel myths and to embrace hard truths from the Bible that could counter any imagination that was not true.

The pastor wrapped up the session, concluding it with scriptures and a talk that shared how the postmodern culture in which we live might be letting in the occult/New Age in subtle ways.

The power of pastoral counseling

Perhaps it might be a healthy thing for the newcomer (who either was once directly involved or influenced by the occult/New Age) to attend counseling sessions as a means to get in touch with who he or she is in Christ. This can only strengthen the newcomer's confidence and identity in Christ.

When I did pastoral counseling, I was aware that each newcomer into the church was at a different level of faith. In their book, *The Critical Journey*, Janet O. Hagberg and the late Robert A. Guelich state that faith has stages of growth to it.[16] Counseling helps people to recognize not only who they are, but also where they are in their faith. According to Hagberg and Guelich, those with whom we interact on our faith journey can teach us to determine what and how we experience any phase of our faith.[17]

I am convinced that counseling sessions can prevent many from dropping out of the church and going back to their old life and friends. For so many, isolation has been a way of life prior to coming to Christ. The counseling sessions help them integrate with other church members.

PRAYER STRATEGIES

THERE ARE SOME BASIC prayer strategies for both the psychic or occultist/New Ager and the church member to take. The church members, in loving the newcomer, might pray that the newcomer will feel welcomed and loved. They might ask the Lord to show them details of how to make the former psychic/New Ager feel welcome, with invitations, acts of kindness, and words spoken to them.

The former psychic or occultist/New Ager might ask the Lord to give him or her a love for their new family in Christ—and with it, new confidence and boldness not to sit back, but to get involved. As well, they might ask the Lord to show them if there is anything they can do to enter their new church with more peaceful confidence.

If you happen to have loved ones who need prayers (so they will go to church or adapt to the church they attend), pray that they find the counseling help they need within the church. As the lady in chapter seven encouraged me, "You have everything to gain from your new life in Christ and church family!"

TALKING IT OVER

1. What are the differences between psychic and prophet?

2. Have you seen any abuses in the church? What might they be? What would you say (if you could) to those doing them?

3. Let's say that you are the pastor of a church where some newcomers have come in and you hear they are psychics and practitioners of the occult. After they come down and give their lives to Christ, *how would you follow up?* What class or counseling sessions would you offer them?

4. As a pastor or church leader, what would you do within your church to educate and inform your congregation about the occult/New Age to make them aware of newcomers who have either practiced it or been influenced by it through culture? How would you as a pastor inform them of the dangers, while at the same time not creating a "witch hunt" atmosphere?

5. Think of various ways (as many as you can) to integrate a former psychic or occultist/New Ager into the church. In this exercise, groups can be formed, with groups taking one or several "ideas" assigned by a leader and exploring those ideas within each group. This leaves creative potential for discussion, reports, and role-playing.

6. Have individual groups list as many subtle ways as they can how the culture might be influencing people with occult and New Age perspectives and practices.

≈

CHAPTER 9

THE HOPE OF
HIS CALLING

The eyes of your understanding being
enlightened; that you may know what is the hope
of His calling, what are the riches of the glory of
His inheritance in the saints.

—EPHESIANS 1:18

MY JOURNEY

I READ THE LETTER that had just arrived in the mail. It
was from a major Christian university seminary. It spelled
out a long list of things I had to do and qualifying tests I
had to take to be accepted into the university. I had not
been to school in more than twenty years, much less taken

any test! "Am I nuts to do this?" I thought. Then the seminary was expecting me to write an essay on ministry and my background. "Oh dear! Now I know I am in over my head!" And it was calling for recommendations from professors! Most of my former professors had passed away.

"Oh, Lord," I prayed, "give me confidence and strength to pursure my dream of attending seminary!"

To escape my fears, I busied myself with the assembly of our fragile, silk Christmas tree. As my fingers worked through the entanglement of knotted wires, strings, tape, detached branches, and cords, I felt my mind gradually freed of all worry about the impossible task of applying to seminary that loomed before me. As the mess in my hands was gradually transformed into a miracle of lights, I began to see clearly how the hand of God, my Creator, was on every detail of my journey, no matter how knotted or entangled things appeared. So how could I fail?

Several years have passed. I now have my masters of divinity with honors, and my doctor of ministry. I cannot help but reflect how the Lord called me and qualified me, giving me favor all the way through the years of schooling to make it happen. I write about this because if He can do it for me, He can certainly do it for you, too!

His faithfulness provides uncommon favor

Once I came to Christ, my eyes were opened to the hope of His calling. Once in Christ, I discovered that He was faithful to my calling, which was really His calling for my life. His Word assured me of His faithfulness: "He who calls you is faithful, who also will do it" (1 Thess. 5:24). As I began to walk out His calling for my new life in Him, I discovered something else—uncommon favor. You can find that as well! Here are the areas in which I found it:

He makes a way

One area of uncommon favor was through the Lord making a way for me to go to school. He made a way for His calling on my life to be fulfilled. I was required to attend graduate school (seminary), but I had to fly at least once a month from Orlando, Florida, to Tulsa, Oklahoma. How in the world could I do that on such a tight budget? We were just getting by!

Here is how the Lord made a way. Quite often there would be an announcement at the airport from the check-in counter: "Ladies and gentlemen, we are in an oversold situation. If you would like to give up your seat and ride on another carrier, we will give you either a free airline ticket or a voucher." The voucher was usually for four hundred to six hundred dollars. The announcements came every time I traveled. Needless to say, I learned to spring to the front counter like a pole-vaulter! It was not unusual for me to pick up free trips and vouchers toward trips every time I traveled to school. In fact, on one trip, I picked up three free flights. I applied them to upcoming school trips. As part of the uncommon favor, I often got placed on the next flight out, which was first class. But why should that surprise any of us? Does God's Word not promise us this blessing?

> Now to Him who is able to do exceedingly abundantly above all that we ask or think, according to the power that works in us.
>
> —EPHESIANS 3:20

He provides all our need

Another area of uncommon favor was where the Lord made provision. He miraculously met all of our needs for school and living expenses. But why should that come as a surprise? His Word has promised us:

> And my God shall supply all your need according to His riches in glory by Christ Jesus.
>
> —PHILIPPIANS 4:19

When I was at school, there were hotel and meal needs, not to mention books and supplies and incidentals and just plain living expenses on the home front. Because seminary was in another state in another region of the country (with colder weather at that), I often needed different clothes to fit the weather needs that were different from Florida. Also, since I was attending seminary, I needed more specific conservative clothing—like dresses or skirts or nice slacks with blazers. My needs were great. But I found out that my God was greater, and He was able to supply all my needs!

How did the Lord provide all of our needs? Financial aid covered the books. Extra work came through a publisher who offered Terry some freelance design projects. Extra cash came from the same publisher for me to do light copywriting. From time to time, each and every month, we would get a note from a relative with ten or twenty dollars to encourage us. God was in our face, showing us that He was meeting day-to-day needs down to the finite detail!

"Watch Me work!"

Often, the Lord performed a miracle that took my breath away. When I first started school, I was required to have a computer to do my papers at home and on the road when at school. So on a budget, Terry and I put aside small amounts each week, saving for this much-needed laptop. Then on a Friday morning (the weekend when I was to buy the computer for my Sunday trip to Tulsa), we had a dental emergency that wiped out everything from our computer fund. No computer! What was I to do?

Terry and I got on our knees and prayed. As soon as we finished our prayer, I heard that still, small voice in my spirit, telling me: "Sandra, watch Me work!" I conveyed this message to Terry, and within minutes, our phone rang. It was the pastor for whom Terry was working. He told us that the Lord had spoken to him minutes ago, telling him I needed a laptop for school! Now there was no way that he knew this, because neither Terry nor I had ever mentioned this to him or his wife. This was truly the Lord fulfilling a specific need miraculously. When the Lord speaks to you, "Watch Me work!" get ready for your miracle!

REFLECTIONS

OVER THE YEARS, I have come to realize that when God calls you, He calls you regardless of your past. He calls you regardless of your present financial constraints. He calls you regardless!

I have found that not only does He call you regardless of limitations and circumstances, but perhaps because of them! Do not misunderstand—God does not need dark pasts to validate His call. However, He will use what you have been through for you to be an even more compassionate and better witness to those who are going through the same things! He will let you convince those people that if He can bring *you* from those things, then He can bring them through those things as well! If He can bless you with a miracle, He can bless them! So your struggles—if you let them—can be the "regardless of" testimonies that show people that regardless of what you face, God can make a way for you! There is hope of a great calling that awaits once you or your loved one have accepted Jesus Christ as Lord and Savior!

Let the apostle Paul (who was Saul at the start of Acts 9) be a model of one who had a bad past—a past of persecuting Jesus. Saul gave his life to Christ, and he was transformed and given a new name—Paul. Regardless of Saul's past, the Lord transformed him into Paul and gave him a miraculous future to do the work of the ministry. Throughout the Book of Acts, you can see that Paul's calling was not without resistance, trials, and persecution. But regardless (that *regardless* word again), Paul's calling was greater than the present-day trials he faced. His God was greater than the obstacles and people that came against him. In fact, Paul was so favored by the Lord that a way was always made for him to do his ministry and fulfill God's calling for his life. If God, who is no respecter of persons, did it for Paul, He can do it for you and me!

God's Word confirms this truth:

His calling is His ministry for you.

Then Peter opened his mouth and said: "In truth
I perceive that God shows no partiality."

—ACTS 10:34

If God has made a way and shown uncommon favor
to others, then why can't He make a way and meet all of
our needs? As we walk out His calling on our lives we
are, in essence, bringing about His ministry. Think about
that. So why wouldn't He make a way to meet all of our
needs for His ministry to happen?

WHAT CAN BE DONE?

PERHAPS YOU HAVE A loved one or know of someone
who in some way is under some of the dark or New Age
influences of our postmodern culture. They might not be
practicing any occult or New Age, but by living a life void
of Christ, they might be naturally "living and breathing
in" a culture that is often against Him or void of Him.

What do you do? How do you point to the glorious
calling of God that awaits your loved ones once they come
to Christ? Do you point instead to hell, which awaits
those who reject Him?

There is always something you can do to minister,
not just hope in Christ for eternity (salvation), but also
the hope of His calling for them. As the Holy Spirit gives

us wisdom in all things, He will give you the insight and direction you need in guiding your lost loved ones to the Lord. (See John 14:26.)

Again, what do you do? Keep praying and encouraging your lost loved ones that God has something special for them. Encouragement and love go further than condemnation against them.

Once they come to embrace the Lord (and salvation), share how God will make a way for them in His great calling on their lives. Share the powerful promise of Philippians 4:19, which says that their God shall supply all their need according to His riches in glory by Christ Jesus. This will truly mean something to your loved ones who will need to be reassured that the Lord is with them in their new walk of His calling!

PRAYER STRATEGIES

THE BEST PRAYER STRATEGY you can take when praying for a loved one who is in the occult/New Age is to pray daily and pray often! Pray words of faith, citing God's Word (see sample prayers in chapter 10). Prayer can—and does—work changes. It works miracles! Never stop and never give up!

FINAL THOUGHT

JESUS HAS COMMISSIONED BELIEVERS to be His disciples who are to go and make more disciples: "Go therefore and make disciples of all nations" (Matt. 28:19). As believers in Christ, each of us has a hope in Him and the hope of His calling.

If you feel that you or a loved one have been influenced or controlled by occult/New Age thinking, just know that the Lord is more powerful than the forces of darkness. Know that as you pray (and continue to pray) that He will honor your prayers and be there. He not only answers prayers, but He performs miracles! He can bring anyone out of darkness—from New Age to new life in Him. Because of this truth, you and your loved ones have everything to hope for and everything to live for!

The Lord not only answers prayers, but He performs miracles!

TALKING IT OVER

1. Consider how you would minister to someone you sense has great potential if he or she would

only come to the Lord. If you have a group considering this question, divide into pairs. Each pair makes up a scene and one person role-plays the part of someone who sees potential and the other person plays the part of the lost loved one who hasn't a clue that God has a calling on his or her life once they come to Jesus Christ.

2. Consider individually or discuss in your group ways in which to point someone (lost in occult/New Age) to a great God who has great plans and purposes for his or her life. Draw upon some possible "bridges" (see chapter 7) that might help that person be more aware of the Lord.

CHAPTER 10

∾

PRAYERS

The effective, fervent prayer of a righteous man
avails much.

—JAMES 5:16

GOD'S WORD TELLS US that we are to bear one another's burdens. (See Galatians 6:2.) All around us are people who need a relationship with Jesus. They might be family, friends, neighbors, coworkers, or strangers. They are reminders of lone souls who are cut off from Christ and reminders that they are human beings waiting for us to meet them on the bridge of connection.

In this chapter are prayers for every specific need. You can tailor them to suit the description and the needs of the person for whom you are praying. These prayers are not to force anyone to Christ, but rather to plant a seed that will grow in that person's life so he will realize that he needs Christ in his life. They need a Savior and they need a friend who sticks closer than a brother. (See Proverbs 18:24.)

Use this chapter not only as one of information, but also as a resource center—much like a handbook—where you can come often and pray for the needs of others. Not only will the prayers in this section bring results in the lives of those around you for whom you pray, but they will also bring results into your own life as you grow stronger in your faith each time you use them.

Remember, it is not what you are doing through prayer, but what the Lord is doing through you, ahead of you, and alongside you to reach someone lost behind a wall that can only be scaled and conquered by a bridge of connection that points to Jesus Christ. In the prayers that follow, insert the appropriate name or names in the blanks.

PRAYER FOR SPOUSE

Father God, in the name of Jesus, the name above all other names, thank You for _____, and thank You for our life and our precious times together. Even

though _____ does not know
You, I still thank You that (he or she) will! We
live in holy matrimony, so I am praying that our
state of holy matrimony be blessed by You as we
pursue it together in You.

Thank You, Jesus, for dying on the cross
for _____'s and my sins.
Thank You that even as I speak, You are
touching _____ and letting
(him or her) feel Your unconditional love. Thank
You for bringing _____ to
salvation. Use me in a powerful way to
represent You. Use me as Your vessel to point
_____ to You. In Jesus' name
I pray. Amen and amen!

PRAYER FOR CHILDREN

Father, in the name of Jesus, thank You
for_____. I pray that You
touch their hearts and bring them to You so
that _____ might receive
salvation and have a relationship with You. I ask
that you melt _____'s heart
so that they will be open to hearing about You
and what You want for their lives.

As a parent, I pray that I might have my physical and spiritual ears open to hear the cries of my children's hearts and discern their concerns and anger and any fears beneath the surface and behind the mask. Make me a more sensitive parent and one who listens and ministers Jesus not only in my words, but also in my actions, bringing _____ to Jesus and receiving Him as Lord with a desire to walk in His ways in a relationship with Him.

In Jesus' name I thank You and receive from You that it is done. Amen!

PRAYER FOR RELATIVES

Father, in the name of Jesus, thank You for _____. Thank You that You are sending people, whether acquaintances or strangers, to minister Jesus to (him or her), meeting (him or her) on the bridge of connection.

Also, I thank You that You give me a sense of appropriate times and words to say to_____ when we talk. As an obedient minister and ambassador of Jesus Christ, I am assured and at peace that when I do meet _____, not only will we connect with each other, but I will also point (him or her) to Jesus Christ. There will be a beautiful and wonderful connection between _____ *and Jesus! In Jesus' name I pray. Amen!*

PRAYER FOR FRIENDS

Father, in the name of Jesus, thank You for _____. *I treasure our friendship, and I thank You that because of this special bond of friendship there is also a special place at the bridge of connection where I can approach my dear friend,* _____, *pointing the way to a loving heavenly Father and the good news of a Savior, Jesus Christ.*

PRAYER FOR NEIGHBORS

Father, in the name of Jesus, thank You for _____, *my neighbor. I pray that in me (he or she) will see the face and heart of Jesus Christ. If they do not know Jesus or have a relationship with Him, they will want to after seeing Him in me.*

I pray that You make me Your instrument, bringing the love and presence of Jesus into the daily lives of my neighbors. I also pray that the neighborhood be a joyous, peaceful, and protected one in Jesus' name. May the neighbors feel welcome, open, and free to share the good news of Jesus Christ. May this be a godly neighborhood where the name of Jesus is honored and lifted up above all other names. In Jesus' name I pray. Amen.

PRAYER FOR COWORKERS

Father, in the name of Jesus, thank You for my fellow workers. I pray that in this bridge situation of common ground with my coworkers I can model Jesus Christ in what I say and do and that they can be relaxed and open to receive reminders of Him! I also pray that as we are bonded together in the same work environment, we are able to meet on the bridge of congenial conversation where I will be able to share suggestions of how loving God is and the good news of Jesus.

I give thanks that whatever I say about Jesus is powerful seed that will reap a harvest now or eventually in lives coming to Jesus Christ and salvation.

Thank You for empowering me in my workplace as Your instrument. In Jesus' name I pray. Amen.

PRAYER FOR STRANGERS

Since you will encounter strangers unexpectedly throughout your day, it might be a good idea to memorize this very short prayer to the Lord prior to meeting them in conversation on the bridge where you find them.

Father, in the name of Jesus, thank You for this situation to point to You and how great and loving a Lord You are. Let this seed I now plant in this person's life bring (him or her) to receiving Jesus as Lord, either now or in Your perfect time. In Jesus' name I pray. Amen!

FINAL PRAYER

Lord Jesus, I yield to You as Your vessel. I ask that You use me as Your instrument—Your messenger—to meet people where they are and point to You as their Savior. Use me, oh Lord, and let my words and my heart be the very expression of Your words and heart in reaching and touching lives. May they come to know You and be transformed into Your likeness. In Jesus' name, amen.

Notes

∽

Chapter 2: Where Do They Come From?

1. Brother Lawrence, revised and rewritten by Harold J. Chadwick, *The Practice of the Presence of God* (North Brunswick, NJ: Bridge-Logos Publishers, 1999), 7.

2. J. Robert Clinton, *The Making of a Leader* (Colorado Springs, CO: NavPress, 1988), 19–20.

3. A.B. Bruce, *The Training of the Twelve* (Grand Rapids, MI: Krege, 1971), 11–12.

Chapter 3: What's a Nice Girl Like You Doing in a Place Like This?

1. Barbara Paulin, *The Path of Promise/Path of Peace* (Virginia Beach, VA: A.R.E. Press, 1995), xxii.

Chapter 4: Pull of the Dark Vortex

1. Russell Alexander Morris, "A Biblical Paradigm for Postmodern Ministry" (PhD diss., Louisiana Baptist University and Theological Seminary, May 2004), 119.

2. George Barna, "Americans Draw Theological Beliefs From Diverse Points of View," http:// www.barna.org/ cgi-bin/PagePressRelease.asp?PressReleaseID (accessed March 16, 2004).

3. Frances Schaeffer, *The God Who Is There* (Downers Grove, IL: InterVarsity Press, 1998), 148.

4. Ibid., 149.

5. James Robison, *The Absolutes* (Wheaton, IL: Tyndale House, 2002), 12.

6. Kevin J. Vanhoozer, ed., *The Cambridge Companion to Postmodern Theology* (Cambridge, UK: Cambridge University, 2003), 199.

7. Robison, *The Absolutes*, 29.

8. James W. Sire, *Why Good Arguments Often Fail* (Downers Grove, IL: InterVarsity Press, 2006), 108.

9. Ibid., 108.

10 Ibid.

11. Leonard Sweet, *Aqua Church* (Loveland, CO: Group Publishing, Inc., 1999), 177.

12. Sandra L. Clifton, "Equipping Parents Who Have Teens Influenced by the Relativism of a Postmodern Culture," (DMin project, Oral Roberts University, 2005), 8.

13. Ibid., 214–215.

CHAPTER 7: WITNESS ON A BRIDGE

1.   George Barna, *Grow Your Church From the Outside: Understanding the Unchurched and How to Reach Them* (Ventura, CA: Regal, from Gospel Light, 2002), 22.

2.   Ibid.

3. Colin Brown, gen. ed., *New International Dictionary of New Testament Theology*, vol. 3 (Grand Rapids, MI: Zondervan Publishing House, 1986), 453.

CHAPTER 8: WELCOME TO CHURCH 101

1.   Andrew Murray, *Abide in Christ* (New Kensington, PA: 1979), 211–213.

2.   Ibid., 217.

3.   Merrill F. Unger, "Prophet," on CD-ROM, *The New Unger's Bible Dictionary Logos Library System* (Chicago, IL: The Moody Bible Institute of Chicago, 1998, c 1988).

4.   Brown, *New International Dictionary of New Testament Theology*, 74–75.

5.   Ibid., 74.

6.   Ibid., 76.

7.   Ibid.

8.   Ibid.

9. Josh McDowell and Don Stewart, *Handbook of Today's Religions* (Nashville, TN: Thomas Nelson Publishers, 1983), 194–195.

10. Ibid.

11. Ibid.

12. Brown, *New International Dictionary of New Testament Theology*, 74.

13. Don Campbell et al., *The Theological Wordbook* (Nashville, TN: Word Publishing, 2000), 297.

14. Ibid.

15. Murray, *Abide in Christ*, 81–82.

16. Janet O. Hagberg and Robert A. Guelich, *The Critical Journey* (Salem, WI: Sheffield Publishing Co., 1989, reissued 1995), 53.

17. Ibid.

TO CONTACT SANDRA

for speaking/preaching

engagements,

or information on the

ministry and church,

please go to

sandracliftonministries.org

or fax

866-206-9501